EXTRAORDINARY ESSEX

by Mavis Sipple

Dedicated with love to
Pete and Sarah

With thanks to
David Scott

Published by Brent Publications 2000
ISBN No: 0 948706 10 4

Printed by Basildon Printing Company Limited
Heron House, Heron Avenue, Wickford, Essex SS11 8DL

CONTENTS

ALONG THE ROADSIDE

There are many small treasures to be found along the roadside; milestones, shoe scrapers, sun faces, odd little plaques denoting some long gone bridge or building.

Firemarks can be found on the first floor wall of some old buildings. At one time, the churchwarden was responsible for fighting any fire in the parish. He was allowed to use the parish pump and enlist the help of any bystanders. Later insurance companies, seeing the potential, started their own fire brigades. Some provided their men with smart uniforms, which gave the job a certain attraction. It also kept them safe from the roaming press gangs. Each company would fix a lead or copper firemark or fireplate to any building they insured. When a fire was reported the men would dash to the scene. If the firemark were that of a rival company, they would stand and watch while the building blazed. If the rival company arrived to put out the blaze they would do all they could to hinder them. They would get in the way or accidentally trip over the leather buckets spilling all the water. This behaviour usually lead to an argument and while the men stood shouting and swearing at each other the house invariably burnt to the ground. If, on the other hand there were no firemark, the rival companies would fight amongst themselves for the privilege of putting out the fire and claiming the fee. While they were quarrelling about who should fight the fire, the house usually quietly burned to ashes.

The Essex Equitable Insurance Society was founded in Colchester in 1802 and bought its first fire engine. Firemen were paid five shillings for every fire in Colchester and seven shillings for fires out of the town. Any passer-by who helped put out the fire was also rewarded. Colchester museum has an excellent collection of ancient fire fighting equipment and a display of fireplates.

An Essex Insurance Society plate is on show in the museum on Canvey Island. The museum, one of Canvey's round houses, was probably a workman's cottage built when Cornelius Vermuyden took charge of reclaiming the land from the sea. The museum houses a collection of fascinating objects from an eel spear to a Queen Anne cradle. Outside, are relics of the old swing bridge that was once the only route off the island, and great wooden drainage pipes dug up on the mud flats.

Sir John Cass Charity post.

Another Dutch cottage on the island dates back to 1621. The Dutch cottage in Rayleigh, also known as the Round House or the Octagonal House, is also over three hundred years old and is still used as a private house.

Other round houses can be found in various parts of Essex, including Finchingfield and Stebbing. Old cast iron boundary posts mark the parish boundaries in many towns. An iron charity post stands by the roadside in West Tilbury. Painted white on the black post is the name Sir John Cass and the date 1868. It is one of several posts that marked plots of land belonging to tenants whose rent was given to the Aldgate School. John Cass founded the school. The money from the rents was to be given to the school but just as he was signing the will, John had a massive haemorrhage and died. The blood stained quill pen he was using became a symbol, the students of the school wore a red quill on founder's day.

A wooden post is all that remains of the burnt oak tree on the borders of Hadleigh and Leigh-on-Sea. It bears a plaque saying, 'Here grew the burnt oak being the ancient bound of the Manor of Southchurch belonging to John Gregory Welch Esq. 1832.'

Eastern Electricity Board workers were puzzled when asked about a rusty metal box, bearing the borough's coat of arms, that is standing on the corner of a Southend Street. It turned out to be an electric switch gear cabinet left over from the days when Southend made its own electricity at a nearby site. A local conservationist Richard Owen offered to restore and paint it. Happily thanks to Richard the council agreed to undertake the work. It is now restored and painted green and cream.

Similar to a gargoyle or grotesque, but found on secular buildings are the weird carvings like the Hag of Felsted. The Hag is carved of wood and wears only a chastity belt. She seems to be supporting the corner of the roof of George Boote's shop. She is said to bear a striking resemblance to his wife. George Boote's house is dated 1596. The sign over the shop says, 'George Boote made this house.'

Whipping post.

Figures like this are supposed to keep out the devil and evil spirits. At Great Baddow there is a corbel of a woman in a scolds bridle, probably put there to warn other women to beware of nagging their husbands or making rash or slanderous remarks. Slanderous remarks, perjury, any kind of anti-social behaviour was punished most severely. The wrongdoer could be clamped into the pillory. This was a punishment used in England until 1837. It consisted of a pair of moveable boards with holes cut for the culprit's head and hands to go through. It was usually erected on a scaffold. The prisoner would be clamped to the pillory while the jeering mob pelted him with stones and rubbish. People convicted of forgery, perjury or libel were condemned to the pillory. From 1816, the only offence for which it could be used was perjury. Inside the church at Good Easter stands a wooden pillory, which until a century ago stood on the village green. The village stocks were similar to the pillory, the victim would have his feet in holes between two great planks of wood. The locals would come to mock and throw things at him. The base of the village stocks has been moved to the churchyard at Little Easton and the remainder stands in the chapel. Another barbaric punishment was the whipping post. This was placed on the village green or some other prominent place. The person to be whipped would be tied to the post, which would spin round rather like a rotary clothesline. It was kept spinning by the blows of a lash. The remains of an ancient whipping post stand with the stocks in the chapel at Little Easton. The old village whipping post and handcuffs now rest in the Parish Church at Little Wakering. There is also a policeman's truncheon dating back to 1783, bearing the George III Coat of Arms.

Before the police force was finally established in Essex, the law compelled each parish to provide a lock-up to house villains and wrongdoers. Great Bardfield's lock up, known as 'The Cage' held six

Inside a dovecote

prisoners. The manacles are still intact on the outside of the door. In Canewdon the lock-up is dated 1775 it contains a whipping post and stocks designed to take three offenders at a time. The lock-up, by all accounts could be quite a sociable place. The villain's friends would come for a chat and bring food and jars of ale, which would be passed through the bars. Luckily the lock-up was often situated close to the inn. The lock-up at Dunmow became redundant when the police station was built. During the depression at the end of the nineteenth century the lock-up was used as a soup kitchen for the poor of the area. Lady Warwick, from nearby Little Easton Manor, sent venison from her estate.

The Electric Palace, Harwich.

At Little Easton one of the few dovecotes left in Essex, can be found. At one time dovecotes were built into castle walls. Only the lord of the manor or the monastery owned them. Later they were built into large houses or farmhouses or even churches. By the time of Elizabeth I, there were over twenty-five thousand in the country.

Dovehouses were necessary as pigeon meat was invaluable during the winter months. Every bit of the bird was used, eggs, feathers for dusters and pillows, even the manure was used as fertilizer and for medicinal purposes, as plaster, cure for gout, a restorative, and a cure for fever. Inside, the dovecote has hundreds of tiny nesting boxes built into the walls. A revolving ladder fixed to a central post was used to collect the eggs from the pigeonholes. The dovecote at Easton Lodge is now used as a museum; the pigeonholes can still be seen along the walls.

It is not so long ago that every town had at least one cinema, often two or three. Now most of them have been pulled down or turned into Bingo Halls or warehouses. Some of the fronts of the buildings have been carefully preserved and it is easy to see how splendid they must have looked in their day. The Regent at Chelmsford still looks rather elegant. With so many of the old cinemas neglected or long demolished it is a rare treat to visit the Electric Palace in Harwich. The

5

'silent' cinema opened in 1911 and closed after forty-five years. The building stood sad and decaying until a group of enthusiasts formed the 'Harwich Electric Palace Trust' and renovated it to its former splendour. You can still go into the door marked 'One shilling' and find the original cinema in all its splendour. Now a listed building it is one of the earliest electric cinemas to survive in the whole of Britain and is virtually unchanged.

Southend's Plaza opened in 1929 in Southchurch Road. A penny bus or tram ride from Southend Victoria Circus. The cinema seated 1,250 was a 'theatre of surpassing beauty being ornately decorated in gold and blue'. Prices were 6d, 9d and 1/-. One memorable night in the thirties, the film caught fire and a local man who played the piano entertained the audience. The audience joined in the singing until the fire brigade declared the apparatus safe and the film commenced. After several changes the Plaza finally closed its doors as a place of entertainment and became an electrical warehouse. Finally it was taken over by the council and has been tastefully redecorated and is used for weddings, concerts and a variety of social functions.

ENTRANCES and EXITS

Many of the doors and gateways around the county have an interesting tale to tell.

The ancient door of St Botolph's Church, Hadstock is thought to be the oldest in use in the country. It dates back to 1020. During repair work on the door, human skin was found under one of the hinges. It is said to be skin of a Dane, flayed alive for some sacrilegious act.

The skin was preserved and taken to the museum at Saffron Walden. At one time cattle hide was put between the door and the hinges in order to protect the wood. However, under Copford's ornate doors, the skin was found to be human, possibly that of a Danish pirate caught plundering the church. It was common practise at one time to publicly flay criminals, poachers and blasphemers. Their skin was nailed to the church door to act as a deterrent to any would-be villain.

The north side of a

Devil's door, Sutton Church.

7

church has always been considered to be the haunt of the devil. Here he wanders endlessly, looking for lost souls.

Until comparatively recently, criminals, the unbaptised and those ex-communicated from the church were buried on the damp north side.

When the north door exists, it is usual, at a christening to leave it open, so when the priest says, "renounce the devil" the devil is able to leave by the open north door.

The south door of Runwell church still carries frightening evidence of the devil. At one time the priest Rainaldus, who had sold his soul to the devil, was leading his band of followers in a black magic ceremony, when suddenly the devil himself appeared. He tried to grab the terrified priest. The congregation fled through the south door closely followed by the priest who pulled the door closed behind him. The Prince of Darkness, so angry at being unable to go through the hallowed south doorway, struck a great blow to the door, leaving a burning imprint of his claws. Not to be outwitted, he squeezed himself through the squint, a tiny unglazed window, put into the wall of the church to allow lepers to watch the service. Once on the outside of the building he slammed shut the outer door and imprisoned the unfortunate priest in the porch. When the frightened parishioners returned with another priest, of Rainaldus there was no sign, except a vile smelling puddle of green steaming liquid. When the steam cleared they discovered a small flint, shaped like a head, all that was left of the hapless Priest. The flint bore the inscription 'the wages of sin is death.' This flint is now on show in the Priory at Southend.

The church has always provided sanctuary for fugitives. If a man fleeing from his enemies reached the church, he would be safe. If the church was locked, he could gain sanctuary by holding on to the iron knocker. One of these sanctuary knockers can be found on the door of the church of St. Mary and St. Lawrence, Great Waltham.

There is a great deal of intricate ironwork on doors throughout the county. The west doorway of St. Peter's Church Colchester is blocked up from the inside but can be seen from the churchyard. Its fine 13th-century wrought-iron scrollwork was probably designed by Thomas De Leighton, whose work can be found in Westminster Abbey. At Waltham Abbey, the main door although modern, is interesting in having a small doorway within the great one, like the eye of a needle, as in 'It is easier for a camel to go through the eye of a needle than for a rich man to enter into the Kingdom of God.' A nearby notice asks God to make the gateway wide enough to receive all who need love and care and narrow enough to shut out envy and pride. The South door of Fobbing church has a wonderful 15th century lock carved from a single piece of oak. While the main door of St Peter ad Vincula, (St Peter in Chains) at Coggeshall, has iron hinges showing a cock crowing at dawn, a star and moon for night time, and a blazing mid day sun for a handle. Inside Chelmsford Cathedral are two very tall narrow doors built into the columns, these are doors to cupboards used as storage for the town players from Chelmsford from the 1570's.

Often passed by unnoticed, whether beautifully carved, of ancient design, intricate forged medieval ironwork or just plain mellowed old timbers worn smooth by thousands of hands over the years, most of Essex's fine doors are well worth a second glance.

Many years ago, before the time of Church registers and marriage certificates, the first part of the marriage service took place outside the south door of the church. The couple would say, "I will," and give the ring in front of witnesses. This is one of the reasons why there was often a porch built onto the south door. The seats along the sides of the walls were for the witnesses. Over the years the porch has taken on many different roles, the benches became a rough bed for vagrants or for any parishioner in need of shelter for the night. The porch was sometimes used as a schoolroom. Rayleigh's sixteenth-century porch was used by the Curate, Thomas Woodruff, as a school for six boys. When the church became the centre of the community the porch was used for important meetings. Serious business such as the taking of oaths and settling of disputes took place in the porch. Prittlewell's porch, and that of Great Wakering, are quite unusual, they have two storeys. The upper room of Great Wakering's porch is known as 'the Priest's Chamber.' It is believed that it was used by monks from Beeleigh Abbey as sleeping quarters when they were preaching at the church. South Benfleet's porch is thought to be the most beautiful in the county and dates back to 1450. The original porch at All Saint's Church Springfield was built from a bequest in the will of William de Wenden. He left 'to the porch one thousand shingle, half a hundred laths and one thousand nails.' He also left eighteen pence to the Sacrist.

On the ceiling of the porch at Coggeshall a large central boss depicts a pelican feeding her young. An ancient legend says that the depicts a pelican feeding her young. An ancient legend says that the pelican pierces its own breast and feeds its young on the blood. Today behind the boss, swallows nest and feed their young. Above the porch is the priest's chamber used for many years to store the church records.

At Dedham's fifteenth-century church the carved porch doors have been cut across, leaving three feet of the upper part fixed. This was done so that an extension across the whole of the western bay could be built. The extra bay was to make room for the many people who crowded into the church to hear the famous John Rogers, or Roaring Rogers as he was affectionately nicknamed. He was a famous and popular character. At his funeral so many people attended the church to pay their last respects, that three times more people crowded into the gallery than it was built to hold. The gallery collapsed under the great weight. Even this disaster impressed the crowd; they were convinced that God had honoured the man with a miracle. Roaring John Roger's memorial can be seen inside the church.

Lich-gates were originally built to shelter the coffin and mourners before they entered the church. Here they waited for the priest to lead them into the church for the service. When they were built they had a central bench or coffin stone on which they could rest the coffin while they waited. In later times many fine lich-gates were built as memorials, or to commemorate great battles or important events. Buried in the churchyard at Dovercourt are many of the thousands of soldiers who died of malaria when they were sent to help Austria fight against Napoleon during the Walcheren Expedition. The handsome lich-gate at the parish church in Dovercourt was presented by Queen Victoria in their memory. In return for this honour the Parish erected a splendidly regal statue of her majesty.

The Reverend Pickles was killed in a car accident at Great Waltham. He had left money in his will for a lich-gate to be built at his church in Topsfield.

Prittlewell's lich-gate, although modern is roofed with very old tiles and is part of a war memorial. Many of these lich-gates are beautifully made and finely carved with loving care and precision. They are works of art in their own right. Another work of art is the wonderful Great Gate House at St. Osyth's Priory. With its fine medieval vaulting it is thought to be the finest in the county. St. Osyth's Priory gets its name from the daughter of the first Christian ruler of the Angles. For

One day the Abbess sent her to fetch a book. Books in those days being handmade were extremely valuable so it was a great honour to be entrusted with the task. As she crossed the bridge, Osyth was swept into the stream by a strong wind. After three days she was seen rising from the water, book in hand. Osyth was betrothed to the King of the East Saxons but she really wanted to remain in the Convent. During the wedding celebrations a pure white stag appeared outside the door of the palace. The groom, unable to resist the chance to hunt this exceptional creature, dashed off in pursuit. Osyth saw her chance and slipped out, ran back to the convent and took the veil. To show his love for her, her new husband forgave her and settled her in a village called Chich, where she built her own nunnery. When the Danish invaders captured Osyth, she steadfastly refused to bow to their gods. They cut off her head. She carried her head to the church. Later she was canonised and the village was renamed St. Osyth.

The largest surviving Roman gateway in Britain is the Balkerne Gate at Colchester. Originally it consisted of two walkways and two carriageways, with guardrooms and towers. The huge buildings were erected around the end of the first century. The gate was built across the road leading to London. It was used by the military, probably as a fort as well as a gate.

Sun and Moon Gateway, Lee Valley Park.

The Abbey gateway at Waltham has two arches, one for pedestrians and one for vehicles. The first church at Waltham was built of timber in the 7th century. An Augustinian priory was built there by Henry II. The priory became an Abbey in 1184. The Name Waltham Holy Cross came about in 1030, so the legend tells. A carpenter from Somerset was told in a dream to go to a hill above his village

11

Somerset was told in a dream to go to a hill above his village and dig. Every night he dreamed the same dream. Finally he and some of the villagers went to the hillside and began to dig. After a while they found a great marble slab, which was broken in two. When they lifted the slab they found a life-sized crucifix with a carved figure of Christ. They also found a bell, a book and a smaller crucifix. Tovi the Proud, Lord of the village, decided to take the cross to one of the religious centres of England. It was loaded onto a cart drawn by twelve red oxen and twelve white cows. The animals refused to move until someone mentioned the name of one of Tovi's great estates, Waltham. At the mention of Waltham the animals began to pull the cart. So the great cross came to Waltham, which was at the time just a clearing in the forest. The followers of the cross founded the town of Waltham Holy Cross. The cross had a reputation for healing and is supposed to have cured King Harold of paralysis. Harold built the Minster as a fitting place to keep the cross.

Another gate at Waltham is in the Lee Valley Park, surely one of the strangest modern gates. To celebrate the fact that Waltham is on the meridian line, zero degrees, in line with Greenwich, the Meridian Gateway was opened in 1995, a huge red and blue sun and moon gate with a starry archway.

There is a strange tale told about an Essex gate and a calf. This story started off the taunt 'Essex Calves.' Many years ago an Essex farmer had a prize calf. Somehow the animal's head became jammed in a five-barred gate. The locals came to help. They pulled and pushed, but still the calf remained stuck. They stood around trying to work out a way to free the animal. Then one bright lad had an idea. He ran to fetch an axe and before anyone realised what he was going to do, with one swift blow he cut off the calf's head. People from the surrounding villages thought this was a huge joke and were constantly calling out to them 'Essex Calves,' a name that stuck for many years. This may or may not be true, like the tale of the wheelbarrow, which was bitten by a mad dog. The villagers took the barrow and put it into quarantine. Or the time that the town band was playing in a room over a pub and a passer-by popped in to say how nice it sounded. The band, highly flattered by this praise, downed instruments and went outside to listen. These, and other unflattering tales are known as 'The Coggeshall Jobs.'

STATUES AND STONES

Although Essex cannot boast any stones as spectacular as those at Avebury or Stonehenge, there are some most interesting stones in the county. For instance the strange pudding stones found dotted around the county have caused a great deal of speculation. Some people say they are ancient milestones, put there by the Romans, others claim they are part of the pagan stones, similar to those at Stonehenge. Some think they were left by the ice age. No one is really sure. They are called pudding stones because they are supposed to look like a giant plum pudding, being a conglomerate of ironstone and small pebbles that look like the currants. The iron often makes them a reddish colour. Many pudding stones have been put into the building of churches and walls since Norman times.

Certain stones were worshipped by the pagans. The church called them devil's stones. At the base of the tower of Broomfield church is strange stone. This big pudding stone was built into the wall, but protrudes out several inches. It is thought to be a pagan Bronze Age relic. It was originally planned to build this church in New Barn Lane but every morning when the workmen arrived they found a dragon had moved the stones down to the Green. Realising they were fighting a losing battle they decided to build by the Green. Close to New Barn Lane a field was named Dragon Foot Field, here pieces of Roman tiles were found. Roman bricks were used in the building of the church. Around the area of Alphanstone Church are a number of large stones, one, built into the west wall of the nave is thought to be part of a bronze age stone circle. Magdalen Laver, North Stifford, Fyfield and Dunmow also have similar stones built into the walls. South Weald has a large pudding stone on the pathway between the church and the lich-gate.

When the villagers of Beauchamp Roding decided to build a church they chose a site near the village. They planned to use the great stone they had found lying in the grass at the top of the hill. They

13

Roman Mark Stone

dragged the huge stone down to the chosen site. The next morning it had gone. They discovered it back at the top of the hill. Undaunted, they dragged it down again. Again the stone returned to the hilltop. After this happened three times, the villagers decided that to build the church at the top of the hill, by the stone was probably their easiest option. Something was obviously trying to tell them where the church should be built. Similar stories are common throughout the county. At Dunmow when the church wall was built a huge stone was left on the outside of the boundary wall. This did not please the stone so it leapt over the wall, so that it could be on Holy ground.

At Newport you can see a huge Leper stone. Tradition has it that it was used for cleaning the money left by the lepers. Others say it was the place the locals left food for the lepers. No one has been able to prove these theories one way or another. Near the porch in Thundersley Church is a strange stone with weird holes in it. This is a Roman Mark Stone. The holes were once filled with oil and a wick. It acted as a primitive oil lamp, rather similar to the rare cresset stone

Staddle Stones at Fobbing.

found at Blackmore. This is a flat stone with cup like depressions that were filled with oil and a floating wick. It would give just enough flickering light for the curate to see his way to the chapel and back.

Waltham Abbey is exactly on a line with Greenwich, zero degrees. In the nearby Lee Valley Park, is a Meridian Stone, made of two granite blocks from the original London Bridge, which was demolished in 1968. The stone has been erected on the line of meridian. Named 'Travel and Discovery', the carvings on the stone show the path of the meridian line through the various countries of the world. The base was designed by the pupils of King Harold School.

Staddle stones, sometimes called saddle stones or rick stones are like giant mushrooms, often used as decorative garden ornaments, their real job is to raise a barn off the ground. A stone at each corner keeps the building high and dry and rat free. A splendid example of rick stones being used for their original purpose is in Curtis Farm Fobbing. Barns were built with the doorway facing the farmhouse kitchen window, so that the farmer's wife could keep an eye on what was going on in the barn. It was a very canny farmhand who could manage to sneak out a pocketful of loot without being seen by the farmer's wife. The strange pudding stone querns, made from local rock were clever devices for grinding corn. They have been discovered in many parts of Essex. The two circular stone are roughly twelve inches in diameter (thirty centimetres) and weigh about fifty-six pounds. (twenty-five kilograms.) The corn goes into a small hole at the top and drops down the chute to be ground in the slightly concave space between the two halves of the quern. Querns were first discovered in the Middle East, it is thought in the Iron Age. When the Romans arrived they brought the idea of grinding corn by a watermill,

Querns.

which could be used by everyone in the area and querns, once common domestic gadgets, were cast aside.

Daedalus the famous Greek, who built the labyrinth and learned to fly with wings made from feathers, is said to have invented the first statues. It is he we have to thank for the many statues around the county. One, a beautiful simple statue in the church at Brightlingsea, depicts the 'Queen of Heaven' with a simple request for her to pray for all those who work in ships. Another, outside the Cathedral at Chelmsford, a modern Saint Peter, complete with fish and a yale type key to heaven keeps watch over the passers by.

Travellers to One Tree Hill's Visitor's Centre in the Langdon Hills, are greeted by a giant snake made from a branch of a tree, and a happy sleeping monk carved from a tree trunk.

All across the county are statues of famous people. Thomas Bata's life-sized figure stands outside the Bata factory, which he founded. All Bata employees lived in the Bata village. It had its own shops, cinema, swimming pool, farm, hotel, and schools. In fact it was a complete village, catering for the needs of the whole workforce. The buildings were based on those at Zlin, Bata's former home. Thomas Bata was killed in a plane crash in 1932; his village is now a conservation area.

Another famous Essex man John Ray has a statue in the garden of the Braintree Museum. Ray was a famous botanist, zoologist and theologian of the seventeenth century. The statue was commissioned by the John Ray Trust, and sponsored mainly by local businessmen. It was unveiled by another famous botanist, David Bellamy.

Nicholas Tindal was born in Chelmsford, his father was a solicitor and his grandfather was one of the early historians of Essex. Nicholas became one of the country's most famous lawyers. Presiding over many famous cases and working for many famous clients, including Queen Caroline. His knowledge of the law was phenomenal. He became MP for Harwich and later was made Solicitor-General. He was knighted in 1826. His statue was put up in Chelmsford's Tindal Square.

There are many statues of Queen Victoria in different poses. But the one at Southend was unique in that, when it was first put up at the top of Pier Hill, the pointing hand, pointed downwards, right into the gents toilets. When this was noticed, the hand was broken off and replaced with a hand pointing out to sea. The join was covered up with a bracelet. The statue has since been moved to the cliff top.

Statues abound our churches, towns and villages. From the imposing statues of Churchill, to the tiny figures around the churches, they have all been made and erected for some special reason, either to beautify the building or to remind us of some great person, or past glory.

AROUND THE CHURCHES

Nearly every church has some small delight, some little relic, special only to itself. The bellows from the old village blacksmith's forge are kept in the church at Finchingfield. Brightlingsea has a small crucifix found in the trenches, and a huge bell clapper. Four smaller clappers are on show in Tendring Parish Church. Ashingdon Church has a model of a Viking ship and a Danish flag. Prince Georg of Denmark presented the flag to the parish when the nave roof was consecrated. The Danes helped to restore the roof.

In the church at Great Waltham stands an overseer's dog rapper. A six-foot long pole, beautifully decorated in black and gold bearing the arms of George III. At one time dogs were allowed into the church with their owners. The overseer would sit by the door and use the pole to beat off any stray dogs. He would also use the pole to chastise any noisy children and to wake up anyone rash enough to doze off during the

Mortar at High Easter

sermon. Sometimes a long dog whip was used for the same purposes.

At High Easter a strange mortar, thought to be Roman, was found. It has been used to repair part of the wall. This bowl has two

18

lips for pouring and swivel handles on either side, allowing it to be tipped in both directions. The underside is hollowed, so that heat can be placed underneath. No one is quite sure what it would have been used for. One suggestion is that is was for molten lead, another that it could have been part of the apparatus used in the making of stained glass windows.

Some churches still have old wind-up barrel organs. The one at Fobbing church can play thirty-six different hymn tunes. It was restored by the late Mr. Smith, who was organist at the church for sixty years. The eighteenth century four-stop barrel organ at Blackchapel near Dunmow has two barrels and can play twenty tunes.

Bomb in Harwich Church

Harwich Church has a collection of wonderful Dutch tiles, with scenes such as Adam and Eve being sent out of the Garden of Eden, Cain and Abel fighting, Noah's Ark, and a collection of contented cows. Also in the church is a bomb that was dropped nearby in 1917. The church of St Michael at Fobbing has a rare vinegar bible printed in 1717. It is so named because in St. Luke's gospel, chapter three, the word vinegar is a misprint, it should have read vineyard. Another vinegar bible was found at Hatfield Broad Oak. There are several of these bibles named after a misprint, in the Breeches Bible, in Genesis the word breeches is used for Adam and Eves clothing instead of the more usual aprons ('they sewed fig leaves to make themselves aprons.') The Bad Bible was printed during the Commonwealth, a printer was bribed to change one word on Acts chapter three. When the restoration came he was fined one hundred pounds. All the copies of the Bad Bible were sent to be burned by the common hangman.

Funeral helmets are quite a common sight in our churches, usually high up on the wall. After his funeral, the knight's helmet was placed over his tomb. Later it was transferred to the church. It was usually a cheap replica, not the original helmet. An ancient iron funeral helmet, probably Elizabethan, hangs in the chancel in Good Easter Church, its carved wooden crest shows the head of a dog. High up under the thirteenth century flint tower of Great Bardfield, hang two helmets and in the chancel of St, Peter's Thundersley, hangs a helmet

Funeral cart.

dated 1500. It is supposed to be that of King Henry VII, who was Lord of the Manor of Thundersley.

In the churches at Broomfield and Coggeshall are ancient funeral carts. The cart at Coggeshall is accompanied by a receipt from William Shave, for making a good elm coffin lined with swansdown pillow and French polished. The whole funeral seems to have cost just over two pounds. William Shave carpenter and undertaker also made picture frames and did wallpapering. Church records make interesting reading. Captain Cook's marriage certificate is in St. Margaret's Church at Barking. At Matching Church we hear of a man named Joseph Petts being struck dead in a tempest at Harlow. At St. Lawrence's Church Upminster records note that a walnut tree was planted in November 1645 and that inhabitants of Upminster amounted to three-hundred-and-seventy people, including women and children.

Fobbing's registers go back to 1539 when 'ye daughter of Steven Sansum' was baptised. A stranger found dead in a pond was buried at Hutton. Other records include the wonderful brasses that still remain in many churches. They show a wide variety of people and there is a lot to be learned from the brasses, not only for the names of the people depicted but the kind of armour they wore, the fashions and accessories. The famous Paycockes whose house now belongs to the National Trust have three brasses in the Church at Coggeshall

Usually found in pre-reformation churches, small stone basins, or piscinas can be quite interesting. They are used for washing the chalice after the Holy Sacraments. The drain is arranged to take the water to consecrated ground without mixing with the ordinary rainwater. Apart from the piscina, Stock church has a roughly crafted fifteenth century stoup, vandalised during the Commonwealth and restored in 1949. Set into the wall of the porch outside the door, a nearby sign is a reminder that the stoup contains Holy Water. The bowl of the lead stoup at Ashingdon was used for many years as a funnel for filling oil lamps.

The outside of the building can often be a source of interest. Sometimes an old ordnance survey mark can be found on the wall. Usually there is some stone, statue or carving of note. Weird grotesques and gargoyles, usually with hideous human or animal heads project from the gutter of many gothic buildings. They are made to carry water clear of the wall. Or they can be placed over a drainpipe and it looks as if they have water gushing from their mouth into a pipe, as at Dedham and Coggeshall. They were designed in rather bizarre shapes to frighten off the devil and evil spirits.

Weather Vanes often have a tale to tell. The cockerel, for example is to remind us that Peter heard the cock crow thrice before he denied knowing Jesus. The weathervane at St Martin's church Chipping Ongar shows St Martin and the beggar. Martin gave half his cloak to a beggar and in a dream saw Jesus wearing the cloak. He became a Christian and asked for a discharge from the army, as he refused to fight again. When he was accused of cowardice he offered to stand between the lines of the two warring armies. He gained his discharge and later became one of the first men who were not martyred, to be revered as a Saint. The fishing boat on the vane at the top of the eleventh century tower of St Peter and St Paul, West Mersea church was erected in 1985.

21

was erected in 1985. The boat is a replica of a Mersea smack. The weather vane at Chelmsford Cathedral is in the shape of a dragon.

Mounting blocks are frequently found by the church wall, a relic from the days when the gentry arrived at church on horseback or in carriages and needed a block to step onto from the high carriage or horse. Mounting blocks can be found at Eastwood, Corringham and St. Mary the Virgin Shenfield where the block is accompanied by a metal tethering ring. They come in various designs. One of the most interesting blocks with five curiously shaped stone steps is alongside the church wall at Bradwell, just a short distance away from St. Peter's on the Wall, or St. Peter ad Murum, built on the coast at Bradwell by St. Cedd, on the wall of the Roman fort 'Orthona.' St. Cedd, the eldest of four brothers was sent to Bradwell when King Sigbert asked for a monastery to be founded in Essex. In 653 AD he sailed from Lindisfarne to Bradwell where he found an old Roman fort. At first as was the custom he built a little wooden church. Later he utilised the stone from the fort to build the chapel. Cedd named his chapel after St. Peter. In 664 Cedd caught the plague and died along with twenty nine of the thirty monks who had come from Bradwell to be with him. One of the earliest places of worship in England, this little chapel on its site by the river became neglected and was used as a barn until 1920, when it was restored. Now the chapel standing dramatically on the edge of the coast is furnished with plain wooden benches, a simple stone altar that was commissioned by the Bishop of Chelmsford and the Roman Catholic Bishop of Brentwood. The three stones set into the altar were gifted from Iona, Lindisfarne and Lastingham. Not so ancient but unique in the county is Little Maplestead Church, one of the four of England's remaining round churches. While in common with many Norman churches, the Apse at Hadleigh church is rounded. Silver End has a thatched church.

Not only ancient parish churches are of interest, some small chapels are very attractive and have interesting histories, while many of the new churches around the county are remarkable and well worth visiting. Sometimes the modern blends well with the old. The thriving churches at Hawkwell and Thundersley have managed to tastefully marry ancient and modern.

PULPITS, PEWS AND FONTS

In 1603 it was ordered that a pulpit should be placed in every church. Many of the finest pulpits were made of oak. Barling church has a fine Jacobean oak octagonal pulpit with a sounding board. Sounding boards were sometimes erected to help carry the preacher's voice to all parts of the building. St. Mary's Church Prittlewell has an intricately carved stone Victorian pulpit, one of only sixty or so in the country. St. Mary's Church Maldon has a fine pulpit carved by Bryan Saunders and erected in 1951 as a memorial to Edward Thomas Baker, who was churchwarden there for twenty-seven years. The carved panels mark his many public interests in Maldon and the county. He was Lord Mayor six times.

There were no seats in the very early churches, the congregation gathered round the preacher. Eventually a few benches were fixed to the walls for the use of the old and infirm. From this we get the saying, 'the weakest go to the wall.' In the fifteenth century fixed seats were introduced and this led to the practise of the Squire and other wealthy families having private pews. These were often those nearest to the chancel; they would also have private pews for the household servants. High box like structure, for privacy and to keep out the draughts would surround the Squire's bench. Occasionally they would put armchairs, cushions, curtains and even stoves inside the box.

During the seventeenth and eighteenth centuries, galleries had to be constructed to provide extra seats for the congregation and three decker pulpits were made. The preacher used the top tier, the reader the next and the clerk sat in the lowest. The parish church at great Waltham used to have a three-tier pulpit. There are two lovely watercolour pictures on the wall. One shows the church as it was in 1861 the other shows the vicar reading the service from the three-tier pulpit. At the medieval timber framed building Blackchapel North End, the three tier pulpit is still in regular use. The chapel is of very unusual design. The

Three Decker Pulpit.

white painted pews still have the high-sided doors. Woodcarvers of old took great pride in their work and finished the top of some bench ends with wonderful carvings of birds, animals, flowers, figures or scrolls. These decorations are known as poppy heads, possibly from the French Poupee meaning doll or figurehead. The best known of these must be those in the church at Danbury. Each pew has a perfect carving at each end. They range from an owl to two girl guides. Great Bardfield has carved poppy heads on the choir stalls and at Dedham church is a commemorative pew to the people of Massachusetts carved with foliage of Virginia creeper, a chickadee, a chipmunk, a cardinal bird and other wild life of the USA. The pew ends in the centre aisle have inset NASA medallions to commemorate the first landing on the moon in 1969. Some of the pew ends at Barking Church have little round holders used to hold candles before the days of electricity.

Some choir stalls have tip up seats, on some of these you can find a small shelf, just big enough to perch on and take the weight off the legs, while appearing to be standing. These seats, are named miserichords from the Latin word for pity which is very appropriate, for services were often very long and the monks had to stand sometimes for many hours. The miserichord gave some relief to the aged. Many miserichords were beautifully carved with flowers, fruit or figures. Some times the carver let his imagination run away with him and he carved humorous scenes, perhaps a man pointing to an aching tooth, or being nagged by his wife, scenes from the home, the hunt or anything from everyday life.

Pew end.

Sedilia, are stone seats that are found in the south side of the church usually set into the wall and often have embroidered cushions. They are used exclusively by the clergy; many are carved or ornately decorated. Brightlingsea's sedilia is plain stone while Runwell's is a particularly fine example of beautifully carved polished wood with three arches.

Robert Fitzwalter was the originator of the Dunmow Flitch at the time of Henry III. Fitzwalter offered a flitch of bacon to the first married couple who could convince a jury made up of all men that they had been happily married during the past year. The annual ceremony takes place at Great Dunmow, but the thirteenth century flitch chair is at the church in Little Dunmow.

Many a small child must have spent an uncomfortable hour sitting upright on the little wooden child's punishment chair at St. Osyth's Priory. But a far worse punishment chair is the ducking, or cucking stool. These have been recorded as far back as the thirteenth-century. They were use to punish scolds, disorderly women or fraudulent tradespeople. The offender would be fastened to a chair, bystanders would jeer and shout abuse at them, or they might be taken to the river or pond and ducked. A ducking stool once stood by the side of the pond in Thunderley Glen, said to be used for ducking quarrelsome women. Ducking stools were used also for women suspected of being witches. The witches pool at Leigh-on-Sea was once used for that purpose. There is still a strong strange influence at work in this pond. Known as Doom Pond, it is said to be bottomless. It was filled in for years but every building put up on the site has fallen down. The last building due to be erected there was never finished; In fact the workmen found it impossible to complete the foundations. The site is still unoccupied except possibly by a witch or two?

Witches were blamed for many things, even for stealing holy water from church fonts. The font by tradition is placed in the west end of the church near the main door, symbolising the first entry of the child into the Christian faith. At one time water was always left in the font, where it was readily available in case of emergency; perhaps a newly born baby or an accident victim needed to be baptised in a hurry. But the holy water, much in demand for witchcraft and black magic rites was always being stolen, so in 1220 it was decided that all fonts had to be protected. Flat wooden covers were made with a bar and staple, which could be padlocked to keep the holy water safe. Frequently, to keep out the dust, a silk or linen cloth was placed between the lid and the water. Over the years font covers became more and more intricate in design and by the sixteenth century huge pinnacled towers were made, richly painted in gold and scarlet and white. These often had to have a rope or chain and pulley to raise them off the font. Rayleigh church has a fine pinnacled cover but the tallest in the county is probably that at Thaxted

After the reformation the 'New Evangelists' decided that the stealing of holy water by devil-worshippers was a myth and covers were removed. Many were ripped out and destroyed. Some Norman fonts still carry the holes where the staples were torn from the rim. One of these, dated about 1430, has the two marks where the original locks had been, can be seen in the church at Stock. At Ashingdon, the early sixteenth century font has a modern lid but marks on the stone show that originally there was a cover on hinges and

Font at High Easter.

secured with a chain. Paglesham church had no font at one time and in the 1430's the parishioners were told they must provide one immediately. The rector gave the present font; the wooden cover is in remembrance of a parishioner who was lost at sea in 1941. Used at baptisms before the reformation, the octagonal font at St. Mary's Church Prittlewell has an unusual chrism niche, which held the salt and oil used at that time in the service. Fonts come in many different designs and shapes, some sturdy and plain, others with intricate involved carvings. High Easter's octagonal fourteenth century bowl is carved with emblems and angels; a rather similar font at Margaret Roding has delicate tracery circling blank shields. Greensted's font is made of wood and replaces the big Victorian one thought to be out of keeping with the rest of the building. The one at Kirby le Soken is a small modern movable wooden font and lid.

There is a story behind many of the fonts around the county, one at Tollesbury, was given to the church by a rather reluctant parishioner, John Norman. It cost him five pounds, a punishment for talking and swearing in church. Written on it are the following words,

'Good people all I pray take care
That in this church you do not swear
As this man did.'

The oldest font in Essex is at Little Maplestead. The roughly carved bowl is said to have been made in the eleventh century. The stone font at Blackchapel is thought to be the smallest in England. One of the most modern is the elegant octagonal font in Brentwood Cathedral, its eight sided shape reminds us that the early Christians thought of the week as eight days Sunday being the first and last day of the week. The top of the font is shaped like a cross and the three steps up to the font remind us that Jesus spent three days in the tomb. Great Warley's white marble font, inlaid with mother of pearl and white marble, has two large bronze angels, one on either side symbolising 'One faith, one baptism.' The church of St. Mary the Virgin at Dedham has an eight sided font made in the fourteenth century. It is decorated with the carved figures. The wooden cover is interesting. It was made in Victorian times by a local carpenter named Barber. The oak timber comes from part of a ship named the 'Royal George.' Around the edge of the cover is a Greek palindrome. Copied from a church in Istanbul. The words which read the same backwards and forwards say,

'Wash mine sin, not my face alone.'

Many fonts have had a chequered life, they have been dug up in fields, used as cattle troughs, door stops and all kinds of strange things. Many have been moved from church to church. Dovercourt's ancient font was discovered in a farmyard near the church, it had been used for years as a cattle trough. The fourteenth century font at St. Mary the Virgin, Shenfield is made of stone brought from Normandy. It has the ancient 'green man' symbol carving, representing unity with nature. It was once removed and taken to a church in Buckinghamshire, apparently the vicar preferred a more modern one. Later it was reclaimed and is now back in its rightful place. The early English font at Coggeshall church was also discarded. The church at Pattiswick gave it away and it was used as a horse trough and a flower planter. Luckily, in the mid eighteenth century, it was given to the vicar and he realised how lovely it was and he restored it and placed it in the church. The bowl of the Norman font at Felsted church is alleged to have been found in the River Chelmer. The medieval font from Hutton church was given away and used as a donkey's drinking trough in the garden of the Rectory. It is now a prized possession at Mountnessing Church.

COATS OF ARMS, HATCHMENTS
AND NOTICES

Coats of arms were originally found on shields. Later they came to be part of the heraldic insignia of families or countries. Royal Arms have been hung in churches since the reformation in the sixteenth century, as a sign that the monarch is the head of the Church of England. When Mary came to the throne in 1553, being a staunch Roman Catholic she had all the Coats of Arms of Henry VIII destroyed. When Elizabeth the first became Queen, the Royal Arms were once more displayed, only to disappear again during the Commonwealth. With the restoration of the monarchy in 1660, Charles II decreed that all Commonwealth arms were to be taken down and replaced with the Kings Arms. Over the door in Ashingdon Church is a   James II Coat of Arms dated 1685. These are rare as his reign was so short, from 1685 to 1688, due to the fact that he had to flee from the country. Plenty, of a later date have survived, some have been carefully restored, and many are on show in churches all over the county. They come in many forms, some very ornate, others quite simple but all of considerable interest. The Royal Coat of Arms of George IV over the door of Fobbing Church indicates that Fobbing is a Crown living in the patronage of Her Majesty the Queen. The Royal Arms of William and Mary in the gallery of St. Peter's Church Colchester is rather unusual, the design was used on the half crown coin for a short time. A quite rare Royal Arms from the reign of George first, can be seen at Hadstock Church. Above the tower arch of St. Mary the Virgin, North Shoebury is a Royal Coat of Arms of George the second. All Saint's Church Maldon has a particularly fine Stuart Arms with the motto 'Dieu et mon droit' (God and my right) and the inevitable Honi soit que mal y pense. (Shame be to him who thinks evil of it.)

Hatchments are large diamond shaped boards bearing the coat of arms of someone who has died. They originated in the Middle Ages as memorials. The heraldic coat of arms was painted on canvas and stretched over a board, which was then displayed outside the house by

29

Arms at Maldon.

the family of the deceased. After a period of mourning it was put on the tomb or in the church. Hatchments give the name and age of the deceased and bear their Coat of Arms. The colour of the background indicates the sex and status of the deceased. The sides are called the Dexter; the left side as you look at it and the Sinister, the right side. The Dexter denotes a man and the Sinister a woman. If the Dexter is black and the Sinister white this shows that the deceased is a man whose wife is still living. If the background is all black it shows that the hatchment belonged to a man who was a widower.

One of the hatchments in Maldon Church is of Mrs Piggott, we know from the background, which is all black that she was a widow. Some of the hatchments lining the walls at Great Waltham Church belonged to the Tuffnell family. Those at Brightlingsea's All Saints Church are of the Magens family. The large one is that of the Magen Dorrien Magens who died in 1848, the last of the Magen family to own the estate, it is a very fine example of Tempera (painting with pigments) painting on canvas. The smaller and not so elaborate hatchment is that of his wife, granddaughter of the Earl of Talbot. Rayleigh Church has one hatchment, in Chigwell there are seventeen. Not a hatchment but a banner, The Noble Order of the Garter hangs in the nave of the Parish Church, Saffron Walden. It belonged to Richard Austin Butler, better known as RAB

Hatchment at Coggeshall.

Butler, Conservative MP who brought in the Education Act of 1944 and did much to bring about the Welfare State. The banner originally hung over Lord Butler's stall in St. George's Chapel Windsor. The sign below reads 'In beloved memory of Richard Austin Butler 1902-1982.'

Signs and notices tell us a lot about life in the past. A notice in the porch of Great Totham church reads 'All seats are free' reminding us that at one time it was the custom to pay for a seat in church. Little Wakering has a notice telling of a grant from the Incorporated Church Building Society for the repair of the church on condition that all sittings be free and that an annual collection be given to the Society. Another states 'The Beadles and Pew openers have directions to find sittings for persons in pews not filled by the renters five minutes after the commencement of divine service, by order of the churchwardens, 1st Jan 1856.' Another, 'To the Glory of God,' tells that Samuel James of St Michael's Frinton on Sea, paid the entire cost of lighting the church by acetylene gas in 1910.

Bequest boards are often found on the walls, inside the church or in the porch. They tell of gifts and bequests that various people have made to charity, the church or the priest. Some of these make fascinating reading and give an insight into the value of money in the past. In

Notice.

Great Totham church a bequest board tell of the benefaction of John Goddeshalf, who left the parish a house and sixteen acres of land out of which ten shillings was to be paid to the Lords rent and one shilling and eight pence to the King and the remainder to the church. A board over the north door of St Peter's in Paglesham tells of John Massu, a wealthy silk merchant from Spitalfields. At the time of the Napoleonic war John was horrified to see that some of the parish's poor families were starving. This upset him so much that he

31

made a yearly gift to the six poor families. In Springfield Church, a grant of £35 was given for restoring the church and making more seats available. Sitting was to be free and 'subject to allotment by the church-warden. Suitable provision being made for the poorer inhabitants.'

Who could fail to take notice of the sign in North Benfleet which says, 'Drive slowly. Innocent animals,' or one on a gate 'if you can't be bothered to shut the gate, don't bother coming in.' A sign over a bicycle shop near Chalkwell Schools in Westcliff-on-Sea. Is one not often seen, James Browning and Daughter.'

Outside Epping station, the beginning of the Essex Way, a plaque, placed there by the Campaign for the Countryside commemorates the twenty-first birthday of the long distance path between Epping and Harwich.

A notice in the garden at Hyde Hall explains the presence of plywood pigs in among the flowerbeds. At one time Hyde Hall was a working farm. The area where the pigs lived was called the Pig Park. Although there are no live pigs now, the name has been retained as part of the history of the Hall.

The Ancient Lights notice occasionally found on the side of a house refers to the rights of light over the adjoining land. The right is obtained by uninterrupted light for twenty years or by written authority. Once legally established no building is permitted that would seriously interfere with the privileged light.

PHONE AND PILLAR-BOXES

Telephone boxes first made their appearance on our streets at the beginning of the twentieth century, mainly at railway stations and post offices. They were of no particular design until 1921 when the first concrete kiosk was made. A competition was held to find a design for a new box. It was to be made of cast iron, the maximum cost was to be £40. The chosen design was by Giles Scott, it was to be made of steel and painted silver. The GPO (General Post Office) made it of iron and painted it bright red. This, the K2 design was the forerunner of the much loved red phone box. Various alterations have been made from time to time, but the basic design remained the same for many years, until eventually vandals made it necessary to change the design. The 'Oakham' walk-in booth was invented. Named 'Oakham,' because its

Victorian lamp box.

was shaped like an 'Old Oak' ham tin. Payphones began to move with the times, they needed to be vandal proof and wheelchair friendly, simple but tough. In the 1990s British Telecom became BT. The new piper livery replaced the old BT livery and the familiar red phone box was gradually disappearing from our streets. Thousands were being sold, some for scrap, others to be used for a variety of bizarre purposes, greenhouses, shower cubicles, fish tanks to name but a few. Some are standing rather incongruously in front gardens. BT is now trying to buy back these red boxes. Originally the red phone box was considered to be rather vulgar and after much public pressure, green booths were placed in areas of outstanding beauty. Suddenly the public realised that the red box would soon red box would soon be extinct. Such was the outcry at the sudden removal of the much loved familiar red box, that about 2000 of them have been declared 'listed buildings' and are safe from the constant demand for change. There are still plenty of these around the county, mostly in more rural areas, their many designs have subtle differences, the crown changes with each monarch, some are taller than others. Southend has seven in the conservation area and one at the end of the pier.

Another much loved object is the red pillar box. These were first introduced into our streets in 1852, but only in towns where there was thought to be enough use to justify the expense. They came in many different shapes, sizes, designs and colours. They varied from place to place but since the 1880s the design has remained virtually the same, with just a few minor changes. Each Monarch has a different cipher. The elaborate design of Queen Victoria and Edward VII contrast with the simple square GR of King George V. Some of the sturdy ER of Edward VIII can be found, but these are quite rare as he was made King in 1936 but reigned for just a short time. He abdicated later the same year in order to marry twice divorced Mrs Simpson.

An old Victorian pillar box in Colchester appears to have sunk into the pavement, it has been in place so long, and the pavement had gradually been built up around it. Occasionally you may come across a box with no cipher at all, these are known as 'Anonymous boxes,' one is in daily use in Southend's conservation area.

Wall letter boxes first appeared in 1857 they were first used in rural areas. They cost a fraction of the pillar box. There are plenty of these old Victorian boxes around the county. One fine example is situated opposite the water tower in Benfleet, others can be seen at Fobbing, Tillingham and Felsted another, in Ashingdon was renovated to celebrate the coronation of Queen Elizabeth 11.

Lamp boxes were made much later, so called because they were made to be attached to the gas lamps that had started to appear on the streets. Made by Handyside the earliest boxes bear the cipher of Queen Victoria and the word LETTERS. These are very rare. The wording was later changed to LETTERS ONLY. There are many of these still in use. Two examples can be seen in the Round House museum on Canvey Island.

A wall box in Rayleigh High Street has a notice on it explain-

Frog post box.

the price of one red rose.

The postmaster at Faulkbourne made a little trap door in his bedroom wall so that when, at the crack of dawn the bag of mail arrived for delivery, he had no need to get up. He just opened the trap door, took the mail and went back to bed. The trap door is still there in the wall.

OBELISKS AND TOWERS

An obelisk, according to dictionary is 'a tapering rectangular stone column with a pyramidal apex.' There are several of these around the county. Perhaps the most well known is the Crowstone, a solitary pinnacle, just a few yards off the shore at Westcliff-on-Sea. The original stone was placed there in 1285. It marked the seaward limit of the jurisdiction of the City of London over the River Thames. This stone was replaced in 1755. In 1837 another large stone was placed beside it. Every seven years the Lord Mayor of London visited the Crowstone. These visits were a time of great celebration in the town, especially for the children, who received sweets and other goodies from the important visitors. The names of the visiting Lord Mayors are carved on the stone. The two stones stood side by side for many years. Eventually in order to preserve it from the ravages of the sea, the smaller stone was moved a couple of miles away to Southend's Priory Park, where it stands on the lawn in front of the ancient Priory.

Under the trees in Rayleigh's bustling High Street can be found another interesting obelisk. Erected in 1908 by the Protestants of Rayleigh and District. The inscription tells us that 'near this spot suffered for the truth Thomas Causton and John Ardeley, they were put to death by Bishop Bonner in 1555.' Robert Drake, minister of Thundersley and William Tyms, curate of Hockley who both perished in the fire at Smithfield in April 1556, are also remembered. The names of these four have been adopted by the nearby Fitzwimarc School, whose houses are named after them.

The great granite column in Brentwood was put up in the memory of Brentwood man, William Hunter. He was a Protestant at the time when Queen Mary was trying to restore Roman Catholicism. William, having taught himself to read, was found in the chapel reading the bible. The vicar and he began arguing about the meaning of communion. The vicar, angered at William's view, reported him to the Lord of the Manor, Sir Anthony Browne, who ordered his arrest. Unable to shake William's belief, Browne sent him to the Bishop of London, Bishop Bonner. Bonner tried to persuade him to renounce his faith, but William was steadfast. He refused to give up his beliefs. Therefore, at just nineteen years of age, he paid the supreme penalty. He was 'committed to the flame,' in 1555. In 1861, at Wilson's corner, near the spot where he was burnt at the stake, the obelisk to his memory was erected by public subscription. It was restored in 1910 after being badly damaged by a fire that raged through the premises of the Wilson's draper's shop. Some great cracks caused by the fierce heat can still be seen on the monument.

The Monument, Colne Park.

The forty feet high obelisk on the cliff top at Southend makes an imposing War Memorial, with it's finely carved wreaths between two colourful banners. Designed by Sir Edwin Landseer Lutyens, creator of many famous, buildings, including the Cenotaph in Whitehall, it was erected by the grateful residents to honour the memory of those who died in the two world wars. The names of these thirteen hundred people are recorded on a tablet on wall of the refractory at the local Priory.

Not actually an obelisk, the huge pillar near Colne Engaine has a story attached to it. Colne Park originally belonged to the convent of St. Botolph, Colchester. It had several owners over the years, including

John de Engine. In 1762 it became the property of Michael Hills. He built the great house and beautiful gardens. When he died most of his property went to a young friend, twenty-two year old Philip Astle on condition that he changed his surname to Hills. Phillip made many alterations to the house and garden. It was he who had the great Portland stone pillar built as a memorial to Michael. The huge ionic style column known at the 'Monument' designed by architect J. Soane was started in 1790. The whole height being seventy-nine feet and was to be completed in six months, thirteen feet two inches to be raised every month. The cost was nearly two thousand pounds. A great deal of money at that time. The pillar, completed in 1791 was surmounted by a big copper urn. In 1987 the urn blew off the column. It was restored by the Essex Heritage Trust and the Soane Museum. When the American airmen were billeted nearby the locals told them about the urn and how it was filled with liquid gold. The gullible Americans believed the story and crept up to the monument one night and began shooting at it, hoping the gold would come pouring out. No gold appeared but the dozens of bullet holes are still there.

Behind Colchester Castle stands another obelisk. It commemorates the death of two officers who died during the Siege of Colchester. Sir Charles Lucas and Sir George Lisle, Royalist Officers, were captured by Lord Fairfax. He offered them their freedom on condition that they promised not to fight again. When they refused he declared them guilty of treason and had them executed. The two men were brought to the castle yard and after a short prayer they were shot. They died bravely. Where the bodies had lain after the execution, no grass ever grew. The grass around grew but there was always the shape of their bodies left on the ground. When the King returned to power, Lucas' brother erected a monument to the two. The inscription read,

'Here lyes buried the renown'd
Sr. Charles Lucas and Sr. George Lile,
Basely
Murder'd by the Ld. Fairfax, general
Of the parliament army.

Fairfax asked the King to demolish the monument. He refused and said, "It shall stand as long as the world endures." Years later it was removed and put in Colchester's St. Giles Church. Also in Colchester, is the great water tower that has been affectionately known as Jumbo almost

Part of Zeppelin.

from its construction. A local clergyman first named it Jumbo after a famous elephant of the time. The elephant was currently appearing in Barnham's circus and was about to be taken abroad and parted from his mate. This caused much consternation throughout the country. Even Queen Victoria made a plea for him, but to no avail. Jumbo and his mate were parted forever. The tower although no longer in use, is still a landmark much loved by the locals. Building the tower started in 1882 using over a million locally made bricks. Since 1987 it has been obsolete. There is still much controversy over its future. Another disused water tower, has for years been a landmark at Benfleet. Being the highest point for miles around, it is ideal for its present use by a tele-communications company and a transmitter for the local radio station. The tower at East Tilbury's St. Katherine's Church is reputed to have been destroyed along with the vicarage during the battle against the Dutch in 1667. The soldiers of No. 2 Company of the London Electrical Engineers decided to rebuild the tower. They also erected an obelisk seven metres high. Unfortunately they were made to pull it down, as the General had not given his permission for it to be built. The tower remained unfinished. A stone on the wall is dedicated to the Officers, NCOs and men of Coalhouse Fort who gave their lives in the Great War of 1914-18 and to commemorate Colonel Gordon of Khartoum.

When a German Zeppelin crash landed at Great Wigborough the crew set fire to it and then marched into the local police station, where they surrendered to the astonished local bobby. The enterprising farmer, onto whose land it fell, charged sightseers for the privilege of taking a look at the remains. He said he would use the money he collected for the good of the soldiers. Part of the Zeppelin was put into the church tower when it was rebuilt.

The elegant twin towers at Mistley were originally intended to stand at each end of the church which had been remodelled in the design of Robert Adams in 1776 and demolished in 1870. They are the only surviving church remains designed by Adams. They were saved when it was decided to make them into a mausoleum. Mistley means the pasture where mistletoe grows.

The great tower of All Saints Church Brightlingsea is ninety-seven feet high. It makes a splendid landmark that can be seen for seventeen miles out to sea. In bad weather Canon Pertwee, one time vicar, would often climb the tower and hang a lamp on the flagpole to guide the fishing vessels safely home. The holes in the tower are thought to have been made by musket balls during the Civil War. It was in this tower that the freemen of Brightlingsea met to elect the Cinque Port Deputy, one of the most ancient of civic posts in Essex. Brightlingsea is the only member of the Cinque Ports outside Kent and Sussex. Layer Marney Tower, built in the reign of King Henry VIII is the tallest Tudor gatehouse in England.

Most of the church towers in Essex are of a square construction, but there are six round towered churches. All Saints Church Maldon's triangular tower is unique.

The ancient Curfew Tower at Barking, was once the gatehouse to a very important Benedictine Abbey the largest in Essex. It formed part of the wall around the abbey grounds. The curfew bell was rung from the tower. The bell was also rung to call the people to church. The town grew up around the walls of the abbey. Most of the townspeople were fishermen, their catch would be taken to Billingsgate. The fishing was controlled by the Lord Mayor of London and the Wardens of the Tower of London. The river provided a living for many of the inhabitants of Barking but it caused a great deal of trouble for the abbey. Right back to 1400 the Abbess had complained about flood damage to the abbey.

Most of Rochford hospital has recently been demolished and is now a housing estate but the towering chimney still remains and has been made a listed building. Part of the old Union Workhouse is also left intact.

The famous seven storey octagonal tower at Walton on the Naze is built of brick and is 80 feet high. Built by Trinity House in 1796, its original function was as a beacon to warn sailors of the treacherous rocks off the coast. Just a few years later, in 1818, the old wooden lighthouse at Harwich was replaced. John Rennie built the present High and Low structures which when properly in line showed ships a safe channel into the harbour. The two lighthouses became redundant due to the changing course of the channel. The nine sided brick High Tower is now a private residence and the smaller ten-sided Low Tower is a maritime museum. England's first lighthouse is thought to have been built by the Romans at Dover. Dovercourt's two iron lighthouses, called leading lights just off the beach were built to replace those at Harwich. They are no longer functional but preserved due to public pressure. They were replace by lighted buoys.

Martello Tower.

The first lighthouse was built on the Isle of Pharos at the entrance to Alexandria. One of the seven wonders of the world the light from its wood fire could be seen for thirty miles. Beacons have been used for hundreds of years. In 1588 beacons were lit all across the country when the Spanish Armada was sighted. They were lit again to celebrate the four hundredth anniversary of the event, and again they were fired all across the world to celebrate the millennium.

41

Being so vulnerable to attack the Essex coast has always needed very strong sea defences. The famous Martello towers were built between 1808 and 1810 to defend the country against Napoleon. The idea came from an ancient tower of stone in the Bay of Martello in Corsica. Eleven of these huge towers were built around the Essex coast. They were one hundred and forty feet in circumference, over thirty feet high, with walls about ten inches thick. Inside were quarters for the men, a well for fresh water and a kitchen. The Redoubt at Harwich, built at the beginning of the nineteenth century is a huge Martello tower. It was once surrounded by a moat and armed with ten guns. Inside is now a fascinating museum complete with cells. Outside is a fine collection of big guns. Jaywick's Tower was built to guard a sluice, which could be opened in the event of attack, and flood the surrounding marshes in the hope of deterring the enemy. Just over the border into Suffolk one of these great towers right on the beach has been turned into a holiday home. The tower at Point Clear houses the Aviation Museum and certainly merits a visit.

There has been some kind of defence against the French at East Tilbury since the earthworks 1402. Later Henry VIII built a blockhouse there. In 1865 General Gordon supervised the building of the present Coalhouse Fort which was more or less abandoned after Napoleon was defeated. The fort is being conserved and restored, mainly by volunteers. Tilbury Fort, just a few miles away is said to be the best example of late seventeenth century military engineering in England. It was built in 1670 and replaced the smaller one built in Henry VIII's reign.

Red Army Sands Fort.

Two groups of Second World War Red Army Sands forts placed at the mouth of the River Thames in 1943 still remain. They have a remarkable history since being abandoned at the end of the war. They have been taken over by pirate radio stations. One has been declared a Principality named Sealand. It has its own currency and stamps and Roy Bates, its self appointed King.

A plaque placed on one of a pair of great concrete blocks on the seafront at Southend tells how it was one of eighteen hundred and four of these blocks. They were constructed in 1940 in case of invasion by the Germans. They were placed in their position in the hope of deterring German aircraft.

Dotted around the countryside are dozens of pill-boxes, built during the war. There is a story that many of the builders commissioned to carry out the work were unfamiliar with the plans and often built them upside down or round the wrong way.

When the threat of nuclear war became a real concern, a chain of concrete bunkers was constructed around the country. They were called Anti Aircraft Operations Rooms. Essex County Council bought the Furze Hill bunker at Mistly in 1963 for £5,250, having cost £500,000 to build. It was to be used as the Emergency headquarters if a nuclear war occurred. Central Government demanded that every county have a similar HQ. With the end of the 'Cold War' these emergency bunkers were no longer required and Essex County Council opened Furze Hill and Kelvedon Hall near Brentwood to the public. Dormitories, telephone exchange radio room, map room, and the communications centre make an excellent and authentic exhibition showing how the bunker would have operated in the event of nuclear attack. A very different way of coping in an attack from the defence methods used at Colchester Castle. There is a story, that Colchester gets its name from Old King Cole or Coel. He was Governor under Roman overlords of the district of Colchester. After a difference between certain tribes and the Romans, Coel sided with his people against the Romans, who besieged the town. Luckily the Roman General fell in love with Coel's daughter and married her. Their son Constantine was born in Colchester and eventually became Emperor.

It is no story that Colchester was once the most important town in England, and that the castle was originally a Roman Temple. When the Romans left, the temple was no longer used and gradually became a ruin. After the Norman invasion, the stones were used to build the great castle with the largest Norman keep in the country. Over the years the castle has had many owners and served many purposes. At present is it a museum containing one of the best collections of Roman artefacts in Britain.

Hadleigh Castle was probably first built in 1230. Henry III granted Hubert de Burg Justicular of England (chief political and judicial officer) a licence to build a castle at Hadleigh in that year. At this time all castle construction had to be approved by the King. The castle was rebuilt about 100 years later in the 1360's by Edward III as a deterrent to the French who made daring raids up the Thames. It had a high continuous curtain (wall) with eight towers and an elaborate gatehouse or barbican. The living accommodation lay at the western end of the interior courtyard. In the sixteenth century the castle was owned by three of Henry VIII's Queens, Catherine of Aragon, Ann of Cleeves and Catherine Parr. By the seventeenth century the castle had become a ruin and since then much of it has been lost by landslide. Hadleigh castle with its wonderful view right across the Thames estuary is still much loved by locals and visitors to the country park.

Rayleigh Mount Castle founded in 1070 by Sweyne of Essex is the only Essex castle to be mentioned in the Doomsday survey of 1080. After being occupied for around 300 years the castle became crown property. Richard II gave his permission for the stones of the castle to be quarried. There is nothing left now of the castle except its magnificent view of the surrounding countryside. The construction of the moated castle at Pleshey was started in the twelfth century. Nothing now remains except a small plaque inscribed with the name Ricardus Rex II. This can be found in the wall of Holy Trinity Church, Pleshey. It is said to have come from the main gate of the castle. At the time of Richard II's reign the Duke of Gloucester was Lord of Pleshey. He planned to dethrone the king. Richard heard of the plot and came to Pleshey. He ordered the Duke to be seized and taken to Calais where he was murdered. All the Dukes possessions, his great wealth and the castle were declared to belong to the king. The castle changed hands many times finally it fell into the hands of Sir John Gates who destroyed the castle and sold the material.

PICTURES, GRAFFITI AND EMBROIDERIES

Before the reformation, the walls of churches were covered with paintings. Most ordinary people could neither read nor write, so the pictures on the walls were their storybooks. The paintings illustrated stories from the bible and showed how people lived in biblical times. The preacher would use these pictures along with those in the stained glass windows, in their teaching of the scriptures. Many of these paintings were covered in whitewash by the Puritans and remained hidden for years until the church was redecorated. When the whitewash was removed, wonderful pictures began to show themselves on the walls.

Paintings in the chapel and south aisle of Great Burstead Church were found to be from about the thirteenth century. Runwell's walls and pillars are bright with pictures. Wall paintings were discovered in the nave of Hadleigh church, covering the walls from floor to ceiling, the Lord's Prayer, St. George and the Dragon, angels, Thomas a Beckett, all painted in brilliant colours. Sadly most of them were lost. As soon as the air reached them they peeled off and were irretrievable. Barling and Little Easton are among the many churches in Essex that have paintings. Many of these have been carefully restored. The magnificent wall paintings at Halstead church are the work of Percy Bacon & Bros., and cost £160 in 1893.

St. Michael and All Angels Church, Copford surely has the most wall paintings of any church in the county. The walls and roof were originally covered by pictures. Many can still be seen, 'the Raising of Jairus' daughter,' is thought to be one of the oldest and most important pictures in the country. Another pictures shows Herod and the Massacre of the Innocents, another shows some knights in full armour, thought to be medieval. One of the knights seems to have three feet and four eyes. These pictures are intertwined with marvellous geometric patterns. The wonderful effects were achieved by painting the outline while the plaster was still wet, then filling in the rest as soon after this as possible. The

Wall painting at Copford.

unusual signs of the zodiac around the chancel arch were uncovered after three hundred years of being hidden. Signs of the zodiac so often associated with fortune telling and astrology were fairly common in churches and used to symbolise certain aspects of Christianity. A Christian festival, an Apostle and a sign of the zodiac was assigned to each month. Other zodiac paintings can be found on the ceiling of Waltham Abbey. These were designed in the 1860s. Also at Waltham is the most incredible 'Doom' painting.

Doom is an ancient word for judgement. Doom paintings were used to remind people of Judgement Day. They were usually placed over the chancel arch. The congregation stood in the nave, which represented the world. The altar represented Heaven, as each person went to receive Holy Communion, he or she had to pass under the judgement painting. This reminded them that they would one day pass from this life to the next and be judged. The doom painting at Waltham Abbey depicts the entrance to hell. The scales of judgement, the seven deadly sins and the joy of those received into heaven by St. Peter. It is fortunate that at one time the Waltham's doom painting was in what was once a chapel belonging to a funeral guild. When guilds were abolished in 1547, the chapel was used as schoolroom and a false ceiling was made. The doom picture was above this ceiling and therefore not, as was so often the case, painted over. Later, when the schoolroom was no longer needed it was made into a Lady Chapel and the painting was rediscovered and restored.

Woodham Ferrers Church has a doom painting over the chancel arch, Christ the judge sitting on a rainbow with his angels. Hell, with a gaping mouth is in the corner. The painting is very faint but the writing underneath is clear enough, stating in bold letters 'Fear God and Honour the King.'

Another form of picture, the stained glass window taken for granted nowadays was originally a vital part of village life, used by the priest as a visual aid. We tend to think that stained glass windows are ancient, but many of the quite new ones are of great interest. For instance the Washington Window was presented to All Saint's Church Maldon by the citizens of Malden, Massachusetts, which was founded by Joseph Hills of Maldon. The window is dedicated to the Memory of Lawence Washington, a loyalist clergyman, at one time Vicar of Purleigh. He was buried in Maldon Churchyard in 1652. He is the great-great-grandfather of George Washington, the first President of the USA.

During the Second World War, Great Dunmow Airfield, on the grounds of Easton Lodge, became one of the main stations for the USA Air Force. In the little church on the edge of the airfield is a reminder of those who made the supreme sacrifice and of those who survived. The men of the 386th Bomb Group 'The Crusaders' formed a close and lasting friendship with the locals. In 1987 Jack Filby, Rector of Little Easton Church, and Colonel Lester J Maitland of the 386th, agreed to establish an American Memorial Chapel in the church at Little Easton. Thanks to the Crusaders and villagers the Chapel was opened and dedicated to the men of the 386th Bomb Group. One of the fine memorial windows, 'The window of Friendship and Peace' shows the British and American flags, the hand of friendship and a service man hand in hand with some of the village children. The 'Window of the Crusaders' shows American air crew preparing for a mission. In the background is the airfield complete with control tower, ambulance, runways and aircraft flying in the missing man formation.

All the stained glass windows of Stock Church were destroyed when a land-mine fell in the churchyard in 1940. The east window, 'Christ in Glory,' by Reginald Bell was put in place in 1948. The restoration work on the church was completed in 1965. One of the windows in St Peter's Church, Thundersley, shows a figure with six toes. In the new part of the church a new window tells of the life of Saint Peter. At Wickford a Masonic symbol is part of a stained glass window.

Dedicated in 1993 in Journalist Corner in Broxted Church is the Hostage Window, made to commemorate the ordeals and release of the British hostages held in Beirut. One of the hostages, John McCarthy, has

Spider window at Saffron Walden.

links with Broxted church. At one time the family lived in the house next to the church. John's mother is buried in the churchyard. The windows are 'Captivity' and 'Release'. The 'Window of Captivity' shows some of the horrific ordeals the hostages had to endure and the prayers being said throughout the world for their release. The bound hands, black balloons, doves, yellow ribbons, the clenched fist all symbolic of different aspects of their time in captivity and the hopes of freedom. The 'Freedom Window' glows with colour, the praying hands, the blaze of publicity and hands shaken in friendship. A lasting and touching tribute to these brave men.

Much much older is the Jesse Window. There are only about ten in the country, and one of them is in St. Margaret's Church Margaretting. In the eighteen sixties, an official from the Kensington Museum inspected the window and dated it as at least four hundred years old. He offered to buy it for one hundred pounds and to give the church a replacement window. Although the church was very poor the vicar refused the offer. Being an enterprising kind of man, he wrote to the newspapers about the window hoping to start a fund for its restoration. This was a dismal failure. So the vicar asked a newly widowed lady of the parish if she would like to restore the window as a tribute to her late husband. Happily she was pleased to do so, and the window was restored. It shows the family tree of Christ, starting with David. From Jesse to Joseph, showing twenty-five figures, including figures of David, Abraham and Joseph. The figures are dressed in the fashion of the Flemish workmen who made the glass. It has been called 'the most perfect specimen of 15th century work in Essex'. It is thought to be the work of John Fludde who was the King's glazier.

Not all interesting windows are found in churches. A large plain wall in Colchester has two full size sash windows painted on it, complete with occupants looking out. Many Georgian houses have wonderful fanlights above the doors. The Minories at Colchester is an excellent example. Fanlights were so called because they were shaped like a fan. At one time, when postmen couldn't read, the address was noted by a picture of the fanlight, these being different in every house in the street. Some magnificent fanlights can be seen, one of the finest being at Mistley Towers. A rare 'spider window' in a 15th century house in Saffron Walden is designed like a cobweb.

The tiny windows high up in some of the cottages in Rochford, were once used to guide the smugglers home to safety as they sailed up the Roach. If there was a light in the window they knew customs men were out of the way. At Woolerstone a cat was placed in a lighted window over-looking the river to inform the smugglers that all was well.

Graffiti is often thought to be a product of modern day society but this is not so. Graffiti was found on walls at Pompeii. Ancient graffiti can be found in the Guildhall in Harwich. Beautifully drawn pictures of sailing ships, gallows, a windmill, a church and various other buildings have been cut into the wood by prisoners when the room was part of the gaol. The Riche Chapel in the Church of Holy Cross, Felsted was made of re-used stones, some of these are covered with rather elegant graffiti, much of it upside down. Some graffiti, as early as the twelfth century, must have

Tollpuddle Kneeler.

49

been scratched by priests as they were the only ones who were literate at the time. Rayleigh church's graffiti is in a mixture of French and English and seems to be part of a song, complete with notes. Ancient magic symbols and Solomon's knots have been scratched on several places at Little Waltham. Ancient writing on the wall of Halstead Church record the names of several important people of the parish. There is also a scribbled message that seems to read: 'John Worth, let be your nice legs.'

The days of faded brown velvet kneelers in church are long gone. Now most churches proudly display lovingly embroidered hassocks showing a great variety of subjects. Many, like those at Greensted church could be called an art form in themselves, but two, kept for special occasions are very unusual. They depict the Todpuddle Martyrs, six Dorset farm labourers who were transported to Australia for seven years for campaigning for better wages. They were forced to work in chain gangs and were sold for £1 each. This caused such a public outcry that eventually they had their sentences reduced. They were granted leave to live in Greensted. Later they emigrated to Canada. The story is told on two kneelers joined together with thick rope and used mainly at wedding ceremonies.

A set of beautifully embroidered cushions adorn the seats of the choir stalls in the chancel of Holy Trinity Church, Rayleigh. They were designed by the late Kenneth Cotton, organist at the time and made by the ladies of the Rayleigh Parish Needlework Guild. Started in 1957 they took ten years to complete. They show the history of Rayleigh town and church. St. Andrew's church Hornchurch, has three hundred kneelers of various designs including an R.A.F badge, a reminder of the Battle of Britain pilots and crews from the nearby aerodrome during the war. Behind the altar at Fobbing church hangs a magnificent patchwork cloth, which was sewn by hand by some of the ladies of the congregation. Glory is the name given to the wonderful patchwork cloth behind the altar of Chelmsford Cathedral. The cloth is made up of thousands of coloured crosses.

The wonderful Maldon Embroidery took three years to complete. It was worked by eighty-three embroideresses. This Millennium Embroidery is on show at St. Peter's Tower in the High Street. It was made to celebrate the thousand-year anniversary of the 'Battle of Maldon' in 991. The forty two feet long embroidery shows the history of the town and surrounding area from the coming of the Vikings, the Battle of Maldon, right up to the present day Maldon. It depicts the mace presented to the first Mayor, the heavy traffic in the High Street, the coming of the railway and lastly the signature of all the embroideresses.

CHESTS AND BELLS

Chests and bells are two of the most cherished possessions of numerous churches. For hundreds of years bells have been rung to call people to worship, to celebrate weddings, to ring in the New Year. They have rung to warn of danger, proclaim good news, and mournfully toll at times of sadness or danger.

Most of us like to hear the joyful ringing of the church bells but not the Reverend Nolan, vicar of Prittlewell at one time. He was not at all pleased to hear the bells, especially when they were rung without his permission. The bell-ringers however were great enthusiasts. They rang the bells long and often. Eventually the Reverend Nolan became so annoyed with them that he decided to put a stop to their activities. Armed with a carving knife, he climbed into the belfry and cut all the bell ropes. Then he called the police and told them to go to the church and keep out the ringers. The bell-ringers were furious. Not to be thwarted, they broke the rectory window, climbed through, up to the roof and into the belfry. This infuriated the vicar even more; he fetched his pistols and began firing at the ringers. Finally the local constable arrived and restored order. The bell-ringers were fined. One of the ringers, James Beeson, refused to pay. He was sent to prison for thirteen weeks. Some of the parishioners clubbed together to pay his fine and he was finally let out after swearing an oath that he would not harass the vicar again. The parishioners of Prittlewell hated Rev. Nolan so much, that on November 5th they burnt his effigy instead of that of Guy Fawkes.

Large bells have been used in churches, cathedrals and monasteries around the country since the seventh century. They are usually made from bell metal, an alloy of tin and copper. Transporting heavy bells from foundry to church was difficult on the narrow unmade roads, so they were often cast close to the church. The name Bell Road, or Bell Field is occasionally found near the church and indicates that this is the place where the bells might have been cast. Occasionally, as far back in time as the Middle Ages, silver coins were added to bells when they were cast. No one is sure why this custom persisted. It may have been from a Pagan belief that silver kept out evil spirits or it may have been to ensure a better sound.

The greatest bell in the world is the 'King of Bells,' which weighs nearly two hundred tons. It is preserved as a national treasure in the Kremlin, Moscow. The largest in the United Kingdom is 'Great Paul' at St Paul's cast in 1881 and weighing nearly seventeen tons. Big Ben, Westminster is over thirteen tons in weight. The oldest bell in Essex is probably that in St. Margaret's Church, Margaretting

There are three bells, dated 1577, 1799 and 1847 in the weather boarded tower of Stock Church, the magnificent tower dates back to 15th century and stands separate from the rest of the building on it's own weight, having no foundations. High up in the belfry is the Green Man, with protruding tongue and bulging eyes, said to represent the sins of the flesh.

All Saints Church Maldon originally housed three bells; they were replaced in 1699 by six, two more were added in 1922. The inscription on the old bells says:-

'When first this steeple three did hold
They were the emblems of a scold
No music then, but now shall see
What pleasant music six shall be.'

Two bells were removed from Brightlingsea Parish Church during the religious troubles and another was taken away to help pay for the repair of the nave roof, leaving only one bell left in the huge tower. The one remaining has a Latin inscription which translated says, *'I am sweet as honey and am called The Bell Michael.'*
Bells were often given the names of Saints.

Ashingdon Church has just one single bell. At one time there were two but one was taken. Rumour says that the Lord of the Manor demanded one bell from each church in the area to be sold. The proceeds were to be used to repair the sea wall. He took the bells but the sea wall was not repaired. A local farmer sold all but one of the bells from the church at Foulness. He said it was to pay for repairs to the sea wall. The local witch was so angry at his actions she put a curse on him. The curse was that his land should be overrun by mice.

Two bells were removed by force from Hawkwell's parish church by Sir William Stafford, supposedly to repair the sea wall. The single bell rung at present has the inscription' Thomas Mears of London 1806. Thomas Mears also cast the larger of the two bells at St. Mary the Virgin, North Shoebury.

Bell cage.

The two oldest bells in Holy Trinity Church Pleshey date back to the fourteenth century. They have fairly recently been restored and re-hung. One has the inscription,
'O Virgin Mary pray for us,' the other
'I Thomas, when I sound it is in praise of Christ.'
An interesting dedication on the bells of Tendring Parish church, whose four bells were melted down and made into six reads: -
*'Four Tendring bells had served three centuries through
Then hoarse with age but still with Tendring true
Their metal gave in six to ring anew.'*
This year, as a celebration of the millennium the bells were restored and rehung.

At Mistly and Wix the bells are outside the church in wooden cages. At nearby East Bergholt, just over the border into Suffolk a similar cage outside the church houses five bells. The cage was built in 1531 as a temporary home for the bells. The tower was built with the help of Cardinal Wolsey, whose family lived nearby in Ipswich. The tower was never finished as Wolsey fell out of favour with Henry VIII and was ousted from power. Thus the bell cage remained. It has been

53

moved once, in the seventeenth century. The sound of the bells annoyed the family at the nearby Hall, so they were moved to their present position. East Bergholt is the only place where bells are rung by force of hand. The heaviest five bells being rung by hand in England. They are left in the upright position because, due to their not being counterbalanced it is extremely difficult to get them to that position.

At Andrew's, Hornchurch there are eight bells, two inscribed *'to the Glory of God and to commemorate the twentieth century,'* another, the Wedding Bell has the inscription,

'In wedlock bands all ye who join with hands and hearts unit
So shall our tuneful tongues combine to laud the nuptials.'

There are also two bell ringers ale pitchers. One is dated 1731 and has the names of the bell ringers of the time. The other is larger and was made by Mr Cove. He had a pottery nearby. The jars have passed through many hands over the years, fortunately ending up back in the church.

One of the two bells on show at Prittlewell Priory, used to hang in Rochford Market Hall and later in the Corn Exchange. It was cast by Thomas Bartlett at Whitechapel. Bartlett bells are quite uncommon as many were destroyed in the Great Fire of London. The huge bell standing outside the museum is thought to be from Newgate prison. In 1604 Robert Dow a London merchant 'In his Christian charity, pitying the poor miserable estate of the condemned prisoners who even at their execution were careless of their soules health, jesting and deriding their imminent danger died reprobate.' In the hope of reforming some of these poor prisoners Robert paid for the great bell to be tolled by a man specially appointed to come to the prison at midnight before an execution and distinctly and solemnly ring a bell and to 'pronounce in a lowde Voice. "Ye prisoners within, condemned this day to dye, remember your sinns, call to God for grace while ye have time. And in the morning when they are in the cart, he shall remind them the great bell tolls for you." The bell was rung from six o'clock in the morning, to remind the people that the execution had taken place. After the demolition of Newgate, the bell was taken to Southend at a cost of £35, plus £3 carriage. For many years it was the sole bell at Trinity Church, Victoria Circus. It was moved to the Priory when the church was demolished to make way for redevelopment.

54

At one time one of the most important pieces of furniture in any household was a wooden chest, often given to the bride on her marriage as part of her dowry. Some of these fine chests have found

Ancient chest at Rayleigh.

their way into our churches, often they have been bequeathed in a will. The law of 1503 required that every parish church provide a chest for storing church registers, valuables, and all important parish documents. Many of these chests are still in immaculate condition, and they are of an amazing variety.

The gnarled old oak church chest cut out of a solid tree trunk at Great Bursted is probably from the 12th century, it is supposed to have been used for the collection of money for the crusades, while the chest at Newport doubles as a portable altar. The beautiful chest at Great Wakering Church once held all the parish records, which are now on computer for the benefit of researchers into family history. The huge chest at Brightlingsea still shows the adze marks from the carving of its lid from a tree trunk, and the great iron straps stand proud of the lid, caused by the unseasoned wood shrinking. One of the most ancient, a small dug out chest made from a single block of oak probably over eight hundred years ago can be seen in the parish church at Rayleigh; it still has the original three locks and fastenings. One key would be kept by the Rector and the other two by the churchwardens, all three had to be present when the chest was opened. There is also an iron ring through which a chain would have been threaded so that the chest could be fastened to the wall. Originally it would have been used to store paper and books belonging to the Parish, but later about 200 years after it was made a hole was cut into the lid so that it could be used to collect alms for the poor."

The 500-year-old chest at St Martin's Church, Little Waltham, is dug out from a whole sycamore tree trunk. Paglesham's rather plain but very ancient oak chest is believed to have come originally from Milan. Although considerably patched up and renewed it incorporates timbers, which may be as early as the thirteenth century. It would have been used for storing valuables, documents, plate, and parish records. The medieval brass bound chest at West Hanningfield is over eight feet long.

When they were filled with the church treasures it was very difficult to move the large chests, so many of them were fitted with rings so a pole could be inserted into the rings, and carried by several men.

The parish was responsible for everyone within its boundary. Every person born in the parish had a settlement certificate, which stated they were legally settled there. This was their most important possession. People asking for help had to show the settlement certificate. If they could not produce a certificate they were liable to be escorted to the boundary and made to walk back to their own parish. One copy of the settlement was kept in the parish chest, which was required to have three strong locks. Keys were given only to two churchwardens and the priest. The chest could therefore be unlocked only when all three were present.

A small beautifully worked 15th century almsbox with three hasps for padlocks and two keyholes, stands in Felsted church. Great Warley, the Art Nouveau Church, has a very modern walnut alms box with a shaped top and a pewter sereph on the front. It is used for the collection of contributions. The oak iron-bound alms box near the door at Runwell Church is said to be early Stuart. For a time it was missing from the church. Purely by chance, the Archdeacon mentioned that a Stuart alms box, described as 'rubbish from Runwell' was lying in a sale room at Chelmsford. It was among sale of the effects of the late Vicar of East Hanningfield. It was restored and returned to the church by a Mr Kemble. At Broomfield Parish Church is an intricately carved Bible box, made to hold the rare bible that was given to the church in 1723 by Sara Atwood. The bible was given to Sara's grandfather by King Charles the first. It was lost for a time, and luckily was found at an auction at the vicarage and returned to the church. For safety reasons the bible is no longer kept inside the box.

Not actually a chest but more of a cupboard, the aumbry is where the Holy Sacrament if kept. Many aumbries are beautifully decorated, one in particular in Epping Church is set in blue marble and studded with semi-precious stones. The outer door is made of brass and bears the 'Pelican of Piety' symbolic of the sacraments, the blood of the pelican is used to feed the young. A Victorian niche in the wall has been converted to house a wonderful gilded aumbrey in Stock Church.

Many churches display their chest as a prized possession, in others they have to be searched out. Sometimes covered with a cloth and used as a table or hidden away in the bell tower or vestry. Invariably they are works of art, labours of love, painstakingly made by craftsmen in an age when there was time to linger over the perfection of these everyday objects.

Not all the interesting chests are found in churches. Armada chests are quite common and can be found in many museums. A splendid example is kept at Southchurch Hall, and another at the Priory near Southend. They are made with a most intricate locking system and often have a secret key hole hidden in the lid. These were use as strong boxes, mainly in solicitor's offices for the safe keeping of legal documents.

The witch's chest in Southchurch Hall, once belonged to Cunning Murrell, born James Murrell in 1780, seventh son of a seventh son. James set up business as a cobbler and shoemaker in Hadleigh. He was said to have the power to counteract the designs of witches, stop the evil eye, and to discover thieves and their loot. A keen herbalist, astrologer and healer. He used his nostrums to help the love-lorn and bring erring husbands back home. He and most of his twenty children were buried in Hadleigh churchyard.

TIME

Before the days of clocks and watches one simple way to record the passing of time was by using an hourglass. Similar to a giant egg timer they were often found in churches, resting in a wrought iron stand fixed near the pulpit. The hourglass would help the preacher gauge the length of his sermon. When the sand ran out he knew he had been preaching for an hour and would often upend the glass and start again. A preacher would be known as a two-hour man or a three-hour man or even a six-hour man. Most of these hourglasses have become broken or lost but occasionally the wrought iron stand can be found near the pulpit.

Outside the church the preacher would use a mass or scratch dial, these are the earliest kind of sundial, with lines radiating from a central point, to form a circle or sometimes a semicircle. A wooden peg or gnomon was fixed in the centre. When the shadow of the peg fell on a certain line, often marked with a cross, the priest would know it was time to begin the service. Then he would ring the bell to summon the workers from field or quarry. Ashingdon Church has an interesting very primitive service dial. The simple dial has just eight lines. In the centre is a hole which once held the peg. The priest would draw a charcoal mark on one of the lines of the dial to tell him when to begin the mass. St. Andrew's has been a place of worship for over nine hundred years. The view from the churchyard is truly spectacular, from the north you can see far over the River Crouch, past the Danbury Hills almost as far as Chelmsford. From the south, over the estuary, past Southend pier to the Kent coast.

There are many other scratch dials around the county, scored on the stone by priests. Holy Trinity Southchurch, just a stones throw from Southend has one clear circular dial while at Burnham, Althorne and Great Wakering there are several dials together presumably scratched by different priests. At Springfield Church there are five mass dials together by the priest's door.

The most common sundial is the vertical dial, usually fixed to the south side of the church, often above the porch. These were once the only method of time telling. Vertical sundials come in all shapes,

Scratch dial.

sizes and materials. One of the oldest is at St Clement's church Leigh–on-Sea, high above the porch; this plain square stone has been overlooking the Thames Estuary since 1729. East Horndon Church above the busy A127, now sadly one of the redundant churches of Essex has a similar but sadly neglected dial. 1666 is the date of the beautifully gilded lettered dial at Latton church near Harlow. The huge blue and white dial at Southminster dates from 1814. Hatfield Broad Oak has a stone cube above the porch, a two faced dial one facing SE and the other facing SW. St. Mary the Virgin at Newport has a rather unusual metal dial placed at an angle to face south, while at Widdington inside the church is a rare and delicate stained glass dial. The church at Nazeing has a wooden dial while that on Waltham Abbey is of slate.

As well as a scratch dial Althorne has a pedestal dial dedicated to Captain Oates, who died trying to save the lives of his comrades on their fateful expedition to the South Pole. Pedestal dials are usually

One handed clock, Ingatestone Hall.

found in parks or gardens. In the old walled garden at Prittlewell Priory stands a small brick pedestal with a simple plate with numerals, compass and the motto 'tyme flyes.' One of the dials at Hyde Hall Gardens is part of a birdbath the gnomon is in the shape of a bird.

The demise of the sundial came with the advent of the railway. All time had been 'local time,' differing from village to village, but once train travel began, if trains were to run to a timetable, time had to be standardised, so the newfangled 'London Time' came into being. As well as this, clocks had become more reliable, so the humble sundial fell out of favour and into disrepair. Happily more recently the art of sundialling has been revived and many modern sundials are making an appearance. One, a spectacular steel armillary dial consisting of three great steel rings, designed by Wendy Taylor is situated under a roundabout in Basildon. At the opposite end of the shopping centre under a similar subway an enormous compass covers floor and walls. In the Olde Worlde Garden at Harlow's cycle museum a fascinating tiny dial is part of an amusing bicycle sculpture. Saling Hall has a four-ringed sphere, while on the quay near Colchester is a Heliochronometer a mean time dial. There are many unusual and interesting dials around the county in gardens and parks, on pubs and churches. Sadly, they often remain unnoticed by passers by.

Although clocks have been used since the thirteenth century they were extremely unreliable and were often placed near a sundial, which was used to put the clock right. The sundial was used in the sunny weather and the clock when it was cloudy.

St. Andrew's church Ashingdon has a rather unusual clock the diamond shaped dial is made of black slate; the hours are marked with the words EDWARDVS VII REX. Instead of numbers. At the top is the royal arms of King Edward VII and at the bottom the date of his death, 1910. Great Waltham's clock is also diamond shaped, it has the letters VR, Queen Victoria's cipher and the date 1852. Inside Great Totham Church is a large and very attractive clock. It was originally meant to be on the outside of the church but the money ran out so the clock stayed inside. The clock in Dovercourt's church tower was made in 1740 and repaired in 1994, at the same time it was repainted and the mechanism altered to stop the chimes sounding throughout the night. A clock with no face, dated about 1725 can be seen in the belfry at Stock. Ingatestone Hall's lovely clock with a gold and white enamel face has only one hand and the inscription 'Sans Dieu Rien' (without God nothing.) In Chelmsford a restaurant named 'Back in Time' has a clock that goes backwards.

The biggest church clock in Essex adorns the tower at Bardfield. Dedicated in 1912 its dial and numbers are gilded, gold on a blue background, huge on the little tower it was put there to commemorate the coronation of King George V and Queen Mary.

The modern silver ball clock in Basildon's shopping centre has four faces. It balances high above the shops on a long slender pole. Hatfield Broad Oak has a fairly modern clock but the 17th century machinery and old wooden dial are still in existence.

One Thursday in September 1692, an earthquake was felt all over England, France, Holland and parts of Germany. For about a minute the earthquake shook Colchester. St Peter's church tower was so badly damaged that it had to be pulled down and rebuilt. The clock was added to the new tower and later remounted in its present position. The chimes had to be silenced to avoid confusion with the Town Hall clock. Colchester seems to have been vulnerable to earthquakes. In April 1884 an earthquake shook the town so violently that it is reported a tram standing in North Hill railway station was shaken so hard that the driver pitched head-first from the cab onto the line. Fortunately there were no fatal injuries. Many people suffered cuts and bruises and over a thousand houses had to be completely rebuilt, being damaged beyond repair.

Floral clocks graced nearly every seaside town early in the last century but few remain today. One along the cliff top at Southend is still beautifully kept and usually fairly accurate. In Rochford Square the large ornate clock on the Women's Institute Hall was erected by the inhabitants in commemoration of the Jubilee of her Majesty Queen Victoria on July 22nd 1897.

The best collection of clocks in the county is in Colchester's Tymperley's clock museum. All the clocks on show were made in Colchester. The clock at Coggeshall Town Hall once struck eleven when in fact the time was twelve o'clock. Horrified, the people sent out one of the villagers in his pony and trap to find and bring back the missing stroke.

TREES, MAZES HA-HA'S AND GNOMES

Some Essex trees are reputed to have lived more than a thousand years. The oldest tree in Essex, the huge oak at Great Yeldham, thirty feet in circumference, was planted over a thousand years ago.

Planted to commemorate the Battle of Waterloo in 1815, a lone sycamore tree stands at one corner of the top of Colchester Castle. Over the years the tree grew so large that it had to be uprooted, cut down and have its roots trimmed. Finally a concrete plant pot was made for it, to stop it damaging the structure of the castle.

Another lone tree, an immense solitary ash, was once a familiar landmark and gave One Tree Hill its name. The hill rises 267 feet (84 metres) above sea level. A viewing point was originally established on the hill to celebrate the Silver Jubilee of King George V in 1935. When this fell into disrepair it was replaced thanks to the Automobile Association and Essex County Council in 1983. There are few higher points in the county than One Tree Hill; the views from the top are truly magnificent. The viewing point shows the distance from it to various places such as Southend Pier, (12 miles) Margate 43 miles South Benfleet water tower (6 miles.)

Some trees are supposed to have strange powers, elder trees have strong connections with witches, yews are linked with superstitions and folklore. Yews are most commonly found in churchyards, as they were always thought to be sacred and were planted in pagan places of worship. These sites were taken over by the Christians for their churches. In some cases the churchyard was built round the tree which was the only form of shelter in ancient times, before the building of the church was common. At Great Burstead a huge ancient yew spreads

Turf Maze, Saffron Walden.

twenty yards across the churchyard. The yew is supposed to be a magic tree and a symbol of immortality. A yew bough would be placed on a grave or coffin to ward off evil. Yew was used to make longbows. Some farmers refused to grow yews, believing them to be poisonous to cattle.

Trees are often planted as living, lasting, memorials. In Colchester is the 'Avenue of Remembrance,' a memorial to the men killed during the war. A group of trees was planted on Canvey Island, to commemorate the fiftieth anniversary of V.E. and V.J. Days

Not content with nature's shapes topiary, the cutting of trees or bushes into shapes became very popular at one time. It is one of the oldest garden arts. It was started in ancient China and was introduced into Britain by the Romans. Box was the most popular shrub used. The art of topiary largely died out in the middle ages but was again popularised by Charles II. There are some wonderful examples in the gardens of St. Osyth's Priory, weird shaped birds and finely cut bushes can be seen adjacent to the beautifully kept knot garden. Bridge End Garden in Saffron Walden is also well known for its strangely shaped bushes. These are seen to advantage from the wooden viewing platform. Also in Bridge End Garden is one of the few remaining Hedge mazes. The maze was planted in 1838, it is similar in shape and design to the famous maze at Hampton Court.

Saffron Waldon also has the largest turf maze in England. This seventeen-ringed medieval Christian maze is a popular feature on the Common. Its twisting turning pathway winds its tortuous way for nearly a mile. Each twist and turn is designed to give a different view. Every part of the of the path must be walked and no part is trodden more than once. At one time nearly every village had a turf maze, it vied with the maypole as entertainment on festive occasions. Sometimes a maiden would stand in the centre and the village lads would run the maze is an attempt to claim her. There are very few of these mazes left. The exact date of Saffron Walden's maze is not known but it is recorded that it was re-cut in 1699. The cost was fifteen shillings.

The origins of the maze are lost in time, many legends revolve around them. Maze patterns have been found that go back to Celtic times, they were drawn on thresholds and doorways to keep out evil spirits, confuse the devil and ensure fertility. Pagan mazes were taken over by the Christian Church. They were walked, sometimes on the knees as a penance or instead of taking a pilgrimage. They represent-

Maze on grave at Hadstock.

ed the journey through life, with its twists, turns and trials. The centre being the ultimate goal, a place in Heaven.

Hedge mazes came much later and were loved by the Victorians. Sometimes planted with low box hedges and filled in with herbs and fruit bushes, they were at their best when viewed from an upstairs window. There is a well kept low hedge maze in Priory Park, Southend. One of the strangest mazes in the county is to be found in Hadstock churchyard, on the headstone Michael Ayrton, maze maker and sculptor.

Love them or hate them the garden gnome has been part of the British garden scene since 1843 when Sir Charles Isham discovered them in Germany and brought some for his garden in Lamport Hall, Northants. He became enchanted with them. He built a rock garden for them, with ponds, trees, grottoes and waterfalls. It was Sir Charles who began the cultivation of miniature trees and shrubs, to fit in with the size of his gnomes. Quite soon the gnome craze was taken up by Victorian society. These quaint little figures could be seen in the grounds of many great houses. People came for miles to view and admire them. However, once the ordinary people started putting them in their gardens, gnomes went out of fashion with the aristocracy. In fact they became a subject of derision, even banned from the Chelsea Flower Show. Only one of the original Lamport gnomes has survived

Ha-ha at Hylands Park.

and it is insured for well over a million pounds. In recent years gnomes have again become popular, perhaps due to a former Prime Minister having a gnome manufacturer for a father? They have appeared in many a garden, but not often in such profusion as in a small front garden in Rawreth where the collection of gnomes, animals and other fairytale characters take up every available space. In Hockley a giant gnome high up in a tree holds a notice saying 'British Gnome Stores.' Orphan gnomes can be sent to a gnome sanctuary in Devon. Here thousands of gnomes and pixies live peacefully in two acres of woodland, and are visited by many thousands of the public.

Another feature found in the great gardens of the fine houses of the eighteenth and nineteenth century was the ha-ha. The Queen Anne house Blake Hall, and Hylands House Chelmsford have parts of well preserved ha-has. These vertical brick walls are the side of a trench. All that can be seen from the house is a gently sloping bank. They were built to keep the deer from coming too close to the house and damaging the garden. The simple ditch ha-ha is merely a ditch with sloping sides to separate the cattle from the arable land on the house side. Another kind of wall, the crinkle crankle or serpentine wall has a considerable fascination, not only for the name, which the dictionary defines as 'crinkum crankum' full of twists and turns, but for their unusual design. They were built full of twists and turns partly to help protect plants grown alongside them and partly for their strength. There are several in the county, one in Ockendon was found to be unsafe and had to be rebuilt by hand using the original bricks. There is another at Great Yeldham.

PUMPS AND WELLS

The village pump has long ceased to be of great importance in our towns and villages. When piped water became available the pump was scorned and neglected. Luckily some have been saved from the scrapyard, restored and given pride of place. The town pump in the Market Square Rochford was paid for by the townspeople in 1820. It was one-foot square and about eight feet high. Water was free at first but later due to demand being greater than the well could produce, one farthing a pail was charged, or one half penny per yolk. The pump was demolished in 1902. There was great rejoicing in the town. A big party

Pump at Little Wakering.

was organised, services were held in the churches, a bicycle carnival took place, and a bonfire lit to celebrate the demolishing of the old pump.

Tillingham has at least three pumps beautifully painted and cared for. The renovated village pump is dedicated to the memory of Gwendoline May Ward, who loved the peace and quiet of the village, it stands under its own lychgate. Another, a rather splendid, well kept pump was first erected in 1894, rebuilt in 1920 and was in use until 1936. After it was made redundant it became very unkempt but was at last restored in 1989.

The elegant pump on the main street at Great Dunmow once stood outside the Saracen's Head Hotel. In 1786 the authorities decided to remove the pump as there had been complaints that it was a traffic hazard. The locals were against its removal and as soon as the workmen filled in the well with bricks and stones, the locals removed them. The authorities filled it in again, the locals emptied it. Three times this happened eventually the angry protesters cleared the rubble and erected a new pump. The turnpike commissioners and the local constable arrived to remove the local blacksmith's work. Tempers became frayed and a fight broke out. Locals against Authorities. There were several casualties on both sides. After reading the Riot Act the constable arrested a number of men and took them off to the nearest police station. They were kept there until the trial at Chelmsford Assizes. Despite vigorous protests from townspeople who maintained the authorities employed thugs and bully boys. They were all found guilty and sent to prison for between six and twelve months.

In 1800 there was a serious outbreak of typhoid in Prittlewell. Ten people died. The water company was able to provide fresh water and persuaded the villagers to have mains water laid on. The old pump was provided by the parish and part of it is standing at the gates of Prittlewell Park. In the churchyard at Little Wakering is an exact replica of Mary's well in Nazareth. It now provides water for those tending the graves in the churchyard. The well at Hadstock church has been covered with a pump known as St Botolph's well. It is supposed to cure many ills including scrofula and tuberculosis of the neck glands,

The Leigh Society maintains the site of the water supply to Leigh Old Town. This was originally a tank of forty-four hogsheads of water supplied by a conduit from a well situated in Rectory Grove,

About a mile away up the hill. In Dovercourt the Spa was opened in 1854 to coincide with the arrival of the railway, which brought hundreds of people to drink the health giving waters of the Chalybeate Spring, which was known to exist before 1670. It was demolished during World War II when the medical officer of health had suspected the water to be contaminated.

Two huge wooden water pipes were dug out of the mud on Canvey Island, At first they were thought to be coffins but it was late discovered that they were pipes used to drain the sea water off the oyster beds.

By the beginning of the twentieth century horse troughs and drinking fountains could be found on practically every high street. They were mostly put there by the Metropolitan Horse Trough and Drinking Fountain Society. The Victorians were beginning to have a conscience about the treatment of the horses and other animals, they put up these troughs to try to make life a little more pleasant for them. Often there

Horse trough in Hockley Woods.

was a drinking fountain at one end of the trough and a small ground level trough for dogs and smaller animals. When the car ousted the horse, hundreds of cattle troughs were destroyed. Luckily some survived. Rochford's trough which once stood in the Market Square, has been removed to the nearby Hockley Woods, where apparently in Henry VIII's time, red ants were imported as food for the pheasants which Henry loved to hunt. There is a move afoot by some local people to have the trough reinstated to its original position. The trough at Rayleigh still stands in the High Street despite the local authorities who at one time tried to remove it. This caused quite a furore. Letters were written, petitions were raised and finally the council gave in and the horse trough stayed in its rightful place in the High Street. The trough in Maldon's busy High Street was put there in memory of a 'good mother, who lived and died in the town.'

The Victorians loved to put up elaborate water fountains. They built them for every conceivable purpose. The winning of a battle by the British in some distant part of the Empire was quite often celebrated by placing an ornate fountain in a prominent position in the High Street, the park or the playing fields. Details of the battle were usually inscribed on a cast iron plate fixed to the fountain. Also fixed to the fountain would be a big iron drinking cup secured to the fountain with a strong chain,

The huge ornate drinking fountain in Saffron Walden, was shown at the Great Exhibition. It was presented to the town by the Gibson family, on the occasion of the wedding of Princess Alexandra to the Prince of Wales. Epping celebrated Queen Victoria's Jubilee by planting a row of trees and building a rather splendid drinking fountain. A small unusual drinking fountain built into a wall has been preserved in Colchester. The inscription reads *'with joy shall ye draw water.'* Hadleigh Salvation Army celebrated the tenth anniversary of its training Centre this year. Part of the Millennium project was the unveiling of a drinking fountain. The fountain was first erected in 1901 to celebrate the laying on of water from one of the wells. The fountain was used by the farm workers. It has been carefully restored and reopened as a symbol of the new beginning for the Training Centre.

MILLS, PIERS AND BRIDGES

Windmills were part of the Essex countryside for years. Now it is a rare treat to come across one. The first record of a windmill in Europe is around the twelfth century but it is believed that simple windmills were in use in some Eastern Countries as long ago as the seventh century. By the middle of the nineteenth century there were more than ten thousand windmills in England. They were used for mainly grinding grain. Some were adapted for irrigating land, sawing wood, pumping seawater from the land, and various other tasks. Eventually other ways of doing the work of the windmill were invented. Steam mills at some of the ports were able to give whiter flour from foreign grain. So in many areas windmills were destroyed or allowed to rot away. They continued to flourish in rural areas until motor transport became cheap and accessible to all parts of the country. Then they became almost extinct. Fortunately some have been rescued and Essex has a fair number of these. Many are open to the public. There are three kinds of windmill, post mills pivot on a post and are turned by hand to make the sails face the wind. Tower mills are built of stone and just the top, or cap turns into the wind. Smock mills are so named because their shape is rather like a shepherd's smock.

The post mill at Aythorpe Roding has been restored to working order. It was built around 1779 and is the largest of its kind in Essex. Finchingfield's post mill is the smallest in the county. It was built around 1756. Bocking's post windmill is dated 1721. Upminster has an excellent smock mill it was built around 1800. It was in use until 1935, its machinery is still intact. The tower mill at Stock was built at the beginning of the nineteenth century and preserved by the Essex County Council assisted by English Heritage. At one time there were four mills

Windmill at Stock.

standing close together in the area. It is rumoured that three were taken down because there was not enough wind for all four!

Thaxted's windmill, a five-floored tower was last used for grinding wheat in 1907. It is now restored to full working order. The two lower floor house a small museum. The tower Mill in Rayleigh was built of brick with a wooden turning cap, in about 1800. When the miller a Mr Crabb became too ill to attend to the sails, a 24-hour a day job, the owner Mr Brown had the sails taken down, during the work a man fell and broke his thigh. Mr Brown had been involved in a road accident and was confined to a wheelchair. He became very short tempered and often ill-treated his wife. Eric, one of his sons, was serving in the army during the Second World War. Eric was very upset and angry at the way his father treated his mother. Being in the army it was fairly easy for him to acquire an anti-tank mine. He hid the mine under the cushion of his father's wheelchair. Archie, was being wheeled out by his nurse when the mine exploded. Archie was literally blown to bits. The nurse suffered serious injuries. Nineteen year old Eric was found guilty but insane. The mill, the tallest in the county, became derelict but has now been carefully restored and made into a museum. It is open to the public on Saturday mornings.

Another familiar sight at one time was the tide mill. The tide would turn the great waterwheel which in turn would operate the machinery and drive the millstones. The most famous mill in the area,

Treadmill crane, Harwich.

just over the border into Suffolk, is Flatford Mill, one time home of the famous artist John Constable. Battlesbridge Mill now boast that it is the largest antiques centre in the county, with spectacular view from the tea shop on the top floor of the old granary. Thorrington's weather boarded tide mill has been carefully restored to working order. On the Dockyard at Harwich is an ancient treadmill. Built in 1667 it was worked by men walking in the inner of the two wheels, whose diameter is sixteen feet. It is the only example of a two wheeled man operated treadmill in the country. It was still in use during the First World War. Having no brakes, it was difficult to work and accidents often happened. In 1894 two men and a lad were working the crane to move some timber, the two men stepped off to make sure the load had been lifted high enough. The boy was not strong enough to control the crane on his own. It rolled backwards and he was knocked unconscious. The earliest reference to this kind of crane was by the Romans in 25BC. They became common in the Middle Ages but by the end of the seventeenth century they were mainly powered by donkeys.

A much more recent construction was the pier. Southend-on-Sea boasts the longest pier in the world, a mile and a third long. The original pier was built in 1830. It was made entirely of wood and was just half a mile in length. Later it was extended to reach into deeper water and at one and a quarter miles became the longest pier in Europe. A single-track wooden railway was laid to carry luggage, which was loaded into trucks and pushed by hand to and from the end when steamers came in. Occasionally a sail was fitted and wind power was used to help push the trucks along. Later the Local Board bought the pier and fitted a metal rail; horses pulled the carriages and a flat truck. The famous pier has seen many changes and has suffered many disasters over the years. In 1976 fire broke out and destroyed the end of the pier. In 1995 another fire burned down the shore end, completely gutting the bowling alley. The pier is still a great attraction to residents and visitors but is not yet back to its former glory.

The biggest of the Essex Piers is at Clacton. Built in the 1870s when the railway came to the town bringing hoards of holidaymakers. It was once the most used pier in the country. Walton on the Naze has the second longest pleasure pier. The original wooden construction built in 1830 was too short for ships from London and Ipswich to reach. A second pier was built and for a time they vied with each other. Then a fierce storm destroyed the original one and at the turn of the century the second was redeveloped, only to have the end demolished during

Ancient Stony Bridge.

the war for fear of an enemy invasion. It was rebuilt when the war was over.

Unique in Britain, thought to be the earliest bridge in Western Europe is the bridge at Pleshey. The only masonry left from the once great castle. In the Lee Valley Park, Waltham Abbey, Stony Bridge, the

75

ancient pack horse bridge spans the Cornmill stream. At one time it connected Grange Yard which was part of the monastic farm to the east with the gateway and the town. Packhorse bridges had very low walls to enable horses or mules to cross them with packs or bundles at their sides with out hitting the walls of the bridge with their load. The modern bridge that crosses the railway line on the seafront at Leigh on Sea was built to replace the old iron bridge the remains of which can be seen on the cliffs. The remaining stone gives the names of the members of the council, the clerk of the works and surveyor. It states that the Cliff Bridge was opened to the public in 1887. The bridge has always been known as Gypsy Bridge after the first boat used as the headquarters of the Essex Sailing Club, that was moored close by.

A plaque on a bridge just outside Little Easton commemorates Thomas Bowyer, martyred in 1555 for his religious beliefs. Condemned to death by the dreaded Bishop Bonner. A beautiful Tudor bridge crosses the dry moat at Hedingham Castle. It was built in 1496 to replace the old drawbridge.

The viaducts at Brentwood and Chelmsford pale into insignificance beside the hundred feet long brick built Victorian Viaduct straddling the A604 at Chappel with its thirty or so graceful arches. Built in 1832 it is still in use by the railway. Chappel is so named because in 1355 it was allowed to have a small chapel of its own, as in the winter it was impossible to get to the church.

The infamous Dartford Tunnel was completed in 1963, nearly a mile long. At its lowest point it is thirty metres below sea level. The second tunnel was opened in 1980. When the bridge was built to link Dartford and Thurrock, both towns wanted it named after them, so a compromise was reached and the bridge was named The Queen Elizabeth the Second Bridge. It was opened by Her Majesty in 1991.

CEMETERIES, GRAVES AND MEMORIALS

Rituals of burying the dead are almost as old as man himself. Long barrows, standing stones and stone circles are thought to be the burial grounds of the Stone Age people.

Despite the coming of Christianity, people still clung to their pagan beliefs; thus early burials took place in the sacred pagan burial grounds. Rough wooden crosses would be placed over the grave; simple altars were made and put in front of them. Later a shelter was built. These were the first church buildings. In 601 AD Pope Gregory decreed that Pagan temples were not to be destroyed but converted into Christian places of worship. Later St. Cuthbert was granted permission by the Pope to establish churchyards around churches thus ensuring that the living were reminded of their own mortality.

For many years, monasteries were the centres of religious life. Monks travelled out to the parishes from the religious centres. Gradually landowners built their own churches, which is one of the reasons why many churches stand close to the Great Manor House. In the tenth century the practise of enclosing one acre was introduced. Thus the churchyard became known as 'God's Acre.'

At first only priests were buried in God's Acre, then later, lay members were allowed in. The very rich were buried in elaborate tombs inside the church, the poor in simple graves outside. They had no coffin but were wrapped in a simple shroud and placed in the hole in the earth, the bodies were facing east to west. When all the ground had been used up they started again, laying the bodies in shallow graves on top of the previous bodies. The ground around the church became raised. Some bones would be removed to the charnel house or crypt.

Victorian Watch Box.

The old charnel house still exists in some of our churches. St Peter's of Colchester has one, which was built in the early part of the 16th century, only the steps leading to the entrance are now in evidence. In Victorian times, private cemeteries sprang up all over the country, Highgate Cemetery in London being one of the most famous remaining. Later they were taken over by local authorities and are well worth a visit if only to see the great variety of ornaments, urns, cherubs, winged angels and anchors now put there as memorials. One chapel, in Southend, has the most extraordinary appearance, being completely covered with creeper which is at its most spectacular in the autumn when the leaves turn rich red. Wildlife abounds in many cemeteries and churchyards; St. Peter's at Thundersley is no exception. Magpies, jays, squirrels and a huge badger sett can be found amongst graves. Badgers tunnelling through the graves have been known to push bones through to the surface.

Most Essex churchyards have a piece of history hidden amongst the gravestones. It was a common practice in the eighteenth century for bodies to be snatched from graves and sold to medical students to practice on, or to hospitals for research.

The 'Resurrectionists' were paid between ten and twelve guineas per body, sometimes more if the clothes were of reasonable condition. In 1832, Samuel Clarke of Little Leighs was convicted of stealing clothes from a corpse, and transported for seven years. Fear of the grave robbers led people to pay a man to watch over the grave. He would stand all night in the churchyard, or in a watch-box and protect the grave from robbers. A well preserved example of an old solid Victorian stone watch-box stands in the churchyard at Wanstead.

Families who could not afford to pay a watchman to protect their departed, took it in turns to sit by the grave in the cold, damp, eerie churchyard from dawn to dusk until the time when the body was thought to have decomposed enough to be of no use to the researchers. Tapered body stones and huge horizontal stones or ledger-stones were sometimes placed over the body, these being too heavy for the body snatchers to move with ease. It was possible to rent a ledger-stone.

Box or chest tombs are usually found near the door of the church, one of the best known chest tombs is the 'cutlass tomb' in St. Clement's Churchyard Leigh-on-Sea, so named because of the great gashes, slashed, perhaps by the cutlasses of smugglers or press gangs. It is the grave of Mary Ellis; 'virgin of virtuous courage and very promising hopes, who died the third day of June 1609 aged one hundred and nineteen. At Wendens Ambo, William Nicholson, sailor with Nelson on the Vanguard rests. Aged one hundred and four he was one of the oldest men in Essex, but not the biggest, that honour went to Edward Bright, said to be the biggest man alive. Bright weighed over forty-four stones, and he was only five feet nine inches tall. He was a candle-maker and grocer. He had six children. For a bet seven men buttoned themselves into his waistcoat with ease. At his burial in 1750, special apparatus had to be made to lift his huge coffin into the vault at the west end of the nave of All Saint's Church, Maldon. He was just twenty-nine years old. His son, was only half Edward's weight but it still needed ten men to carry his coffin to the church.

It was usual to bury the loved-one in a cotton or linen shroud. To help the declining wool trade, Charles II passed the 'Flannel Act'. It said that people must be buried in woollen clothing. An affidavit had to be sworn at the graveside by a close relative that this was done and a note was made in the parish register. A wit of the time is quoted as saying; *'Since the living would not bear it*
They should when dead be forced to wear it.'

If the law was broken and the body was not buried in wool, a five-pound fine had to be paid. Informers were given a reward, so the family of the deceased, knowing they were breaking the law, often informed on their own relatives before anyone else did. Then they claimed the reward and used the money towards paying the fine.

At Greensted a rough wooden cross stands by the gate, the last resting place of a local man who after a drinking session went back to working with his scythe with disastrous results, and consequently bled to death. Nearby is the most ancient of all the graves at this, the only Wooden Saxon church in the world. It is the tomb of a Bowman from the Crusades.

One of the memorials at Dedham reports a death in the year 1747/8. This is because the Gregorian calendar was being introduced. At the time the year began on Lady Day, March 25th. Dates between January 1st and Lady day were shown with dates for the old and the new year until 1752 when the new style calendar was adopted. In Waltham Abbey a tombstone records a death in 1731/2

It was at Waltham that Harold stopped at the cross on his way to the Battle of Hastings. As he prayed, the figure of Christ bowed to him and looked down instead of upwards as usual. This was taken as an ill omen. After the battle Harold's love, Edith Swan Neck, brought the bodies of Harold and his brothers back to Waltham to be buried. His probable burial place is marked by a simple stone with the inscription 'this stone marks the position of the High Altar behind which King Harold is said to have been buried in 1066,'

The Witchfinder General, Matthew Hopkins, who accused women of being witches if they so much as owned a cat, is supposed to be buried on the very spot where he carried out his evil task. The place is now an animal rescue centre, near Mistley. It is said that Hopkins' ghost has been seen there on many occasions.

When the Zeppelin L32 was shot down in flames in 1916, twenty-two crewmen perished in the fire. They were buried in the churchyard of Great Burstead Church. The site of the tomb can still be seen but the bodies have been transferred to a War Graves Cemetery in Staffordshire.

In practically every churchyard can be found perhaps the most poignant of all, small simple headstones bearing names of private soldiers, airmen, deckhands or ordinary seamen, many aged just seventeen or eighteen, who never returned from fighting for their country. At the doorway of the sadly dilapidated church at North Benfleet, stands a large headstone. Its inscription reads, 'to the sacred memory of John Cole a soldier at Waterloo, who at the celebrated command 'up guards and at 'em, was wounded by a musket ball. He heroically persevered until the victory.' The full quotation 'up guards and at 'em again,' was said by Wellington in 1815. John Cole died at Benfleet in 1836. He gave his medal to the curate, whose last act was to erect the headstone. It was re-cut by the Grenadier Guards Association in 1981.

At St. Andrews Church Rochford we find Alice Fulcher aged 105, just a few yards away from the Rev. Cotton and his daughters Edith aged five and Nora one year one month and one week. One of the most heartrending sights is the children's corner at Great Burstead Churchyard, where the gravestones are shaped like teddy bears and carry inscriptions to tiny babies and small children. A huge curtained tomb in Stanford le Hope is covered with cherubs, bones, books and leaves. Some rather macabre skulls are carved on the headstone of Anne of East Horndon, where it is said, Anne Boleyn's head is buried, and where she sometimes walks on dark misty nights.

Churchyards are fascinating places, not only for the inscriptions to those buried there, slaves, smallpox victims, royalists and sinners, but the incredible variety of memorials from the tiny plain cross, and the much loved Victorian draped urn, to the carved cherubs, winged angels, sundials and bird baths, all thoughtfully planned memorials to loved ones.

Memorials inside the church tell some strange stories. One in particular in Great Waltham Church, that of Peter Curgenven, recounts his adventures and his final demise after undergoing the most horrific operation: 'Having his thigh cut off close to his body'. This was in the days before anaesthetics. 'He bore the traumatic experience with surprising sedateness and unconcern.' Sadly he died a few days later. Also at great Waltham is a splendid marble and alabaster memorial to Sir Richard Everard and his wife Anne, a cousin of Oliver Cromwell. At Dedham church a memorial to Judith Eyre, age thirty-five, tells how she died from swallowing a pin, probably accidentally dropped into a plum pudding.

At Finchingfield we read about William Kempe who wrongly

accused his wife of being unfaithful and vowed to keep peace for seven years, during which he did not once speak. He built seven fishponds in his garden, one for every year of his silence. In 1628, at the end of the seven years he tried to speak to her, and found he was unable to do so. His power of speech had deserted him. He died shortly afterwards at the age of seventy-three.

An unusual memorial in the lovely old Parish Church of All Saint's Brightlingsea is a wonderful frieze of tiles naming the men who lost their lives at sea. Albert Barber aged seventy six, drowned in the harbour on Easter Day 1953. Peter John Hickman aged twenty one drowned off the barge Delceon, St Valentines Day 1962. Sometimes two or three men from one family were lost. David Day aged fifteen was lost with his father off the schooner William of Hartlepool 1872. The tiles were the brainchild of Arthur Pertwee who became vicar in 1872. Arthur Pertwee was, by all accounts quite a character. He was often seen climbing the ninety-seven foot tower on a dark and stormy night to hang out a lantern to help the fishing boats find the harbour. Brightlingsea has always had connections with the sea, the oyster industry being most important. Brightlingsea also proudly boasts of being a member of the Cinque Ports, the only member not in Kent. The elected deputy holds one of the oldest civic posts in Essex.

Close to the railway line between Wickford and Rayleigh are two sad reminders of the First World War. Twenty four year old Captain Alexander Bruce Kynoch and Henry Clifford Stroud lost their lives at midnight on 7th March 1918. They were returning home after pursuing German raiders in the last but one raid over London. Their two aircraft collided in mid-air. Their squadrons were from Goldhanger and Rochford. Captain Kynoch has a simple stone memorial. Captain Stroud's memorial is a full sized aeroplane propeller. The two memorials are in the field where the crash happened. The field was sold later but the piece of land where they came down was not included in the sale but was to be forever held sacred. Captain Kynoch is buried in Golders Green. Captain Stroud has a grave in Rochford Parish churchyard and a memorial inside the church. By the roadside a short distance away Pilot Officer Hodgeson, aged nineteen, a New Zealander in 85th Squadron, died crash-landing his burning Hurricane after managing to avoid landing on the village of Shotgate. A simple stone marks the outstanding achievement of Trevor

Osben of St. Osyth, who single handedly circumnavigated the world in his twenty-foot sloop, Chess.

Leigh-on-Sea being one of the oldest fishing ports in the county, it is appropriate that the church is dedicated to St Clement, Patron Saint of fishermen. St. Clement was baptised by St. Peter. He became Bishop of Rome. There is a story that he met his end by being bound in heavy chains and thrown into the sea. In the church yard is a memorial depicting a small boat caught in a huge wave, a tribute to all those fishermen of Leigh who took their cockle bawleys to Dunkirk in June 1940 to rescue the soldiers stranded on the beaches and in the memory of those who gave their lives.

Memorial at Bradwell.

The airmen from the Bradwell aerodrome who lost their lives in the Second World War would never be forgotten. Thanks to one local lady. After much campaigning for some form of monument it was agreed to put up a memorial to them on the old airfield. A local man designed and made a sculpture of a Mosquito aircraft. This was erected almost in the shadow of the Nuclear Power Station. It remembers 'the 121 members of the Allied forces who, in answer to the call of duty, left this airfield to fly into the blue forever.'

End